*Un*CONDITIONAL

A STUDY *of* GOD'S NEVER-ENDING LOVE FOR US THROUGH *the* BOOK *of* HOSEA

Written by Katy McCown | Designed by Morgan Broom and Jamie Collins
Copyright © 2025 by Proverbs 31 Ministries

WE MUST EXCHANGE *whispers* WITH GOD BEFORE *shouts* WITH THE WORLD.

Lysa TerKeurst

PAIR YOUR STUDY GUIDE *with* THE FIRST 5 MOBILE APP!

This study guide is designed to accompany your study of Scripture in the First 5 mobile app. You can use it as a standalone study or as an accompanying guide to the daily content within First 5. First 5 is a free mobile app developed by Proverbs 31 Ministries to transform your daily time with God.

Go to the app store on your smartphone, download the First 5 app, and create a free account!
WWW.FIRST5.ORG

Dear friend,

Welcome to our study of Hosea. I'm excited to go on this journey with you.

As I studied this book, Hosea's words reminded me of a stretch of highway not far from my house where the road becomes steep and curvy. As you can imagine, it's given drivers trouble for a long time. I've heard stories of people who never reached their destination, and I've seen for myself several tragic scenes with emergency vehicles that gave way to crosses staked in the ground.

Over time, measures have been put in place to try to keep motorists safe. The speed limit slows as you head up or down the hill. Large streetlamps now line the center of the highway in conjunction with a sturdy cement divider.

Because of what I've seen and heard, I try to heed these boundaries. I slow my speed and pay careful attention. Even after countless times going up and down this hill, I try not to grow too comfortable. As my children have started driving, I've warned them about what I know and repeatedly urged them to take the same precautions.

Still, every once in a while, I catch myself speeding around the curve. I always wonder when this happens: *Don't I know better? Haven't I heard the stories? Haven't I seen the scenes? Why do I and others sometimes choose to ignore the truth we know?*

On our journey with Hosea and the nation of Israel, we will find God's people on a similar path: a treacherous, crooked road of sin, or rebellion against their heavenly Father. Warnings of the danger that lay ahead abounded, with caution signs at every turn. In His love, God sent Hosea as a prophet to remind His people about what they had seen and heard from Him in the past and to urge them not to ignore His life-giving instructions and good boundaries.

Sadly, we will see Israel chose not to listen.

Thankfully, we will also see **God loved them anyway.**

Even when His people rejected His protections, ignored His affections and grieved His heart ... God was faithful. He was also just; He did not allow evil to go undisciplined. Yet He never delivered a consequence without compassion, and in the end, His deep love for His people would triumph: *"I will betroth you to me forever. I will betroth you to me in righteousness and in justice, in steadfast love and in mercy. I will betroth you to me in faithfulness. And you shall know the LORD"* (Hosea 2:19-20).

As we begin, I want to tell you at the outset that we will encounter some challenging scriptures as we read Hosea.

I highly recommend you spend time with the introductory content of this guide. Understanding the context of Hosea provides an important foundation and helps us keep our focus on God's love for His people even as we witness His discipline of their disloyalty.

As we head down this road together, let's buckle up and wake up. Let's move through this study alert to God's guidance and eager to respond in obedience. When we do, we will be refreshed, transformed and deeply satisfied by God's never-ending love for us.

IN CHRIST,

Katy

GETTING *to* KNOW HOSEA

The book of Hosea was written by the prophet Hosea (Hosea 1:1), a man appointed by God to speak His Truth. Scholars agree Hosea lived in Israel and prophesied primarily to Israel. Hosea's name means "help" or "helper" and is derived from the Hebrew word for "salvation."[1] In keeping with his name, Hosea was sent by God to open Israel's eyes to their unfaithfulness and sin, in the hopes of leading them to salvation through repentance (turning away from sin).

Hosea is considered one of 12 "minor prophets" in Scripture, whose writings are shorter than the "major prophets" such as Isaiah, Jeremiah, Ezekiel and Daniel. As one of the earliest minor prophets to write, Hosea lived and prophesied during a time known as "the Divided Kingdom" in Israel. After the reigns of King David and King Solomon, the once-united nation of Israel went through a civil war and split into two kingdoms: the northern kingdom of Israel, where Hosea lived, and the southern kingdom of Judah. Scholars believe Hosea's first prophecies began as early as 752 B.C., which would place them during the reign of King Jeroboam II, some of the northern kingdom's most prosperous years. Hosea's prophecies of doom and destruction likely appeared ridiculous to the Israelites at this time; however, their exceptional prosperity would give way to sudden and swift decline.[2]

Scholars are unsure if Hosea prophesied verbally to a present audience, but it is plausible he could have spoken his message in God's temple. This place of worship was located in the city of Jerusalem in the southern kingdom of Judah, though Hosea seemingly lived in the north, so scholars remain unsure of whether he spoke the prophecies or just wrote them.

Other than what we learn about Hosea in the first three chapters of his book, we don't know much else about his personal life. Based on what we do know, through his vivid, pain-filled language and the record of his difficult marriage and family life in the book of Hosea, we can conclude he prophesied with a broken heart. Although he loved the land of Israel, as one scholar notes, "Hosea had the unenviable task of presiding over the death of his beloved nation."[3] Hosea prophesied during the final 30 years before Assyria invaded and defeated Israel in 721 B.C.

TIMELINE *of* EVENTS SURROUNDING THE BOOK *of* HOSEA

The Divided Kingdom

Israel was united when King David reigned from 1010-970 B.C. and his son Solomon reigned from 970-931 B.C. But afterward it split into the northern kingdom of Israel (timeline below) and the southern kingdom of Judah (timeline on the righthand page). Also note that the names of the kings mentioned in Hosea 1:1 are underlined so you can easily identify them.

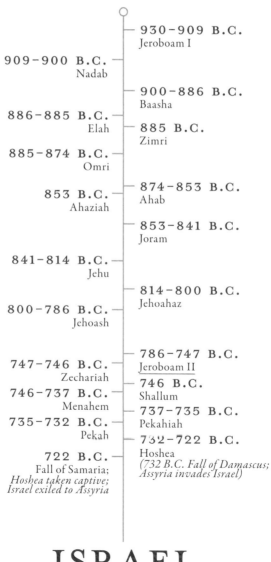

930–909 B.C.
Jeroboam I

909–900 B.C.
Nadab

900–886 B.C.
Baasha

886–885 B.C.
Elah

885 B.C.
Zimri

885–874 B.C.
Omri

874–853 B.C.
Ahab

853 B.C.
Ahaziah

853–841 B.C.
Joram

841–814 B.C.
Jehu

814–800 B.C.
Jehoahaz

800–786 B.C.
Jehoash

786–747 B.C.
Jeroboam II

747–746 B.C.
Zechariah

746 B.C.
Shallum

746–737 B.C.
Menahem

737–735 B.C.
Pekahiah

735–732 B.C.
Pekah

732–722 B.C.
Hoshea
(732 B.C. Fall of Damascus; Assyria invades Israel)

722 B.C.
Fall of Samaria;
Hoshea taken captive; Israel exiled to Assyria

ISRAEL

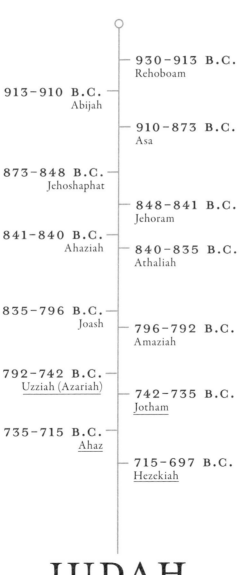

— **930–913 B.C.**
Rehoboam

913–910 B.C. —
Abijah

— **910–873 B.C.**
Asa

873–848 B.C. —
Jehoshaphat

— **848–841 B.C.**
Jehoram

841–840 B.C. —
Ahaziah

— **840–835 B.C.**
Athaliah

835–796 B.C. —
Joash

— **796–792 B.C.**
Amaziah

792–742 B.C. —
Uzziah (Azariah)

— **742–735 B.C.**
Jotham

735–715 B.C. —
Ahaz

— **715–697 B.C.**
Hezekiah

JUDAH

GETTING FAMILIAR *with* HOSEA'S PROPHECIES

THE book of Hosea can be divided into two main sections:

1. Chapters 1-3 describe Hosea's marriage to an unfaithful wife and how it symbolized God's love for His unfaithful people.

2. Chapters 4-14 detail God's response to His people's unfaithfulness, which included both punishment and restoration.[1]

The documentation of Hosea's marriage and family life in Hosea 1-3 has brought up many questions and conversations among Bible readers. Scholars view it in a variety of ways. Some believe it to be purely allegorical, meaning Hosea was speaking symbolically rather than telling a factual story about his real life. Other scholars believe Hosea wrote about two real but separate marriages in the first three chapters of the book: one marriage to a woman named Gomer and one marriage to an unnamed second wife. Still other scholars believe his account is of one marriage (to Gomer) that was broken and then restored. There is no way to know with certainty which of these is the most accurate interpretation of Hosea's marriage(s); we can discern, however, that describing Hosea's family is not the primary point of these chapters. The ultimate focus is meant to be on God and His family. Hosea's marriage and family were symbolic of God's relationship to Israel.[2]

In several instances throughout Scripture, God directed prophets to behave in unusual ways to communicate His Truth in a dramatic and memorable fashion (as you can see in the chart on Page 9). Hosea's marriage was possibly the most extreme example of this in the Bible, as God said, *"Go again, love a woman who is loved by another man and is an adulteress, even as the LORD loves the children of Israel ..."* (Hosea 3:1).

Hosea's action of marrying Gomer and then seemingly taking her back after she violated their marriage was virtually unheard of in the Ancient Near East. According to God's law in the Old Testament, it was wrong for a man to take back his wife after she had married and divorced another husband (Deuteronomy 24:1-4), which Gomer may have done. But as we will see, it was this very fact that drove home God's intended message: In a sense, Israel had divorced themselves from God just as Gomer had divorced herself from Hosea, but in both cases, grace and love ultimately triumphed.[3]

Overall, Hosea's prophecies about Israel are written in roughly chronological order, following Israel through unstable and unpredictable times of political unrest and rampant idol worship. In spite of Israel's worship of the false god Baal, there is evidence that the people also continued their daily sacrifices to the one true God in some semblance of what His law commanded in the Old Testament. They may have had some basic knowledge of God's law, but their obedience was partial and occasional at best. Hosea had the tall order of calling a nation back to a God they didn't really know — a God who loved them, though they certainly weren't showing Him love in return.

SYMBOLIC ACTS *of* THE PROPHETS

Isaiah walked naked through Jerusalem to show how exile would strip God's people.	ISAIAH 20:2-6
Jeremiah's ruined loincloth showed how Judah's pride would lead to ruin.	JEREMIAH 13:1-11
Jeremiah did not marry, which was a sign of grief.	JEREMIAH 16:1-9
Jeremiah went to the potter's house to demonstrate how God is like a potter.	JEREMIAH 18:1-12
Jeremiah broke a jar to show how the disobedient plans of God's people were empty.	JEREMIAH 19:1-13
Jeremiah wore a yoke to symbolize Judah's servitude to Babylon.	JEREMIAH 27:1-22
Jeremiah bought a field to show the restoration of God's people.	JEREMIAH 32:1-44
Jeremiah offered wine to the Rechabites to reveal the unfaithfulness of Judah's leaders.	JEREMIAH 35:1-19
Jeremiah hid stones to foretell Babylon's destruction of Egypt.	JEREMIAH 43:8-13
Seraiah threw Jeremiah's scroll into the Euphrates River to signify the end of Babylon.	JEREMIAH 51:59-64
Ezekiel acted out the siege and destruction of Jerusalem.	EZEKIEL 4:1-5:17
Ezekiel acted out the exile.	EZEKIEL 12:1-16
Ezekiel ate nervously to reflect fear in the land.	EZEKIEL 12:17-20
Ezekiel did not mourn his wife, showing how God would take away His people's delight.	EZEKIEL 24:15-27
Ezekiel used sticks to symbolize the reunification of Israel.	EZEKIEL 37:15-28
Hosea married Gomer to symbolize God's covenant with unfaithful Israel.	HOSEA 1:2-3
Hosea redeemed his wife to symbolize God's redeeming love for His people.	HOSEA 3:1-5
Zechariah crowned Joshua as high priest to point to Jesus, the coming High Priest.	ZECHARIAH 6:9-15
Zechariah acted out the role of shepherd to warn of the dangers of running from God.	ZECHARIAH 11:4-17

ADAPTED FROM "SYMBOLIC ACTIONS OF THE PROPHETS," *FAITHLIFE STUDY BIBLE*. EDITED BY JOHN D. BARRY ET AL., BELLINGHAM, WA: LEXHAM PRESS, 2012, 2016.

HOW DOES HOSEA RELATE TO THE REST *of* SCRIPTURE?

HOSEA AND THE OLD TESTAMENT

THROUGHOUT his writings, Hosea referenced the first five books of the Bible: Genesis, Exodus, Leviticus, Numbers and Deuteronomy, which are also known as the Torah (Hebrew for "law"). These books contain the foundational principles of God's covenant with His people in the Old Testament. God's people had forgotten much about His laws and His covenant by Hosea's time, although it does appear the Ten Commandments were still familiar to Hosea's audience. For example, the wording in Hosea 13:4 (*"I am the LORD your God from the land of Egypt; you know no God but me"*) appears to reference the first commandment in Exodus 20:2-3 (*"I am the LORD your God … You shall have no other gods before me"*).

With the hope of shaking Israel from its stupor of sin, Hosea addressed the crisis of his nation through the lens of Israel's history and traditions, including stories from Genesis and Exodus. From Genesis, Hosea referenced God's dealings with the patriarchs or forefathers of Israel — in particular Jacob, who stubbornly strove to get his own way, even to the extent of striving with God in a physical wrestling match we can read about in Genesis 32:22-32 (and Hosea 12:2-14). Hosea also contemplated the applications of Israel's past exodus out of exile and slavery in Egypt (Hosea 2:15; Hosea 11:1-4; etc.), which happened through a series of miraculous acts of divine deliverance that demonstrated God's love for His people.

HOSEA AND THE NEW TESTAMENT

In the New Testament, centuries after Hosea's lifetime, the Apostles Paul and Peter both drew on Hosea's prophecies to speak to God's people in the early Church. The redemptive love of God, as represented by Hosea's marriage, was an important part of Paul's theology. In his letter to the Romans, Paul referenced Hosea's words as he preached that both Jews and non-Jews (gentiles) can be redeemed by God's grace through faith in Jesus Christ; in Romans 9:22-26, Paul quoted Hosea 2:1 and Hosea 1:10. Peter also pointed to these same verses in Hosea as he urged early Christians to abstain from evil and grow in their faith (1 Peter 2:10).

HOSEA'S WRITING STYLE

HOSEA'S writing will keep us on our toes. His style is oftentimes abrupt — shifting in metaphor, tone or language without warning. For instance, Hosea 12:12-14 reflects historically on Israel's patriarch Jacob, then suddenly prophesies about the future of Ephraim, the strongest tribe in Israel during Hosea's lifetime. One Bible scholar even suggests Hosea was at times intentionally obscure so as to demand the careful ear of his listener.[1] There are many nuances to Hosea's writings that, if we are not prepared, could catch us off guard and confuse us; however, if we pay close attention, we can discover a deeper understanding of God's character and unconditional love for His people.

Below are a few key characteristics of Hosea's unique style that are helpful to know as we approach his prophecies.

METAPHOR

Hosea often used vivid symbolic language to convey intense emotion. Many times he drew on metaphors to paint word pictures. Some examples include the metaphor of Israel as a vine (Hosea 10:1; Hosea 14:7), God as a lion (Hosea 5:14; Hosea 11:10; Hosea 13:7), or God's people as doves (Hosea 7:11; Hosea 11:11). In some instances, Hosea also used the same metaphorical image but with different meanings depending on context: For instance, the morning dew in Hosea 13:3 is an image of human mortality while the dew in Hosea 14:5 is an image of God's refreshing. As noted above, these images often change abruptly in the text. Sometimes Hosea jumps from one metaphor to another, and sometimes a metaphor in one verse is negative, but a few chapters later, the same image expresses something positive.

ORACLES

When reading prophetic books, Bible scholars sometimes break the chapters into "oracles" — specific utterances that are taken as individual prophecies. However, when studying Hosea, it can be difficult to determine where one oracle ends and another begins. Scholars believe this is because the book of Hosea is less like a collection of individual oracles and more like one unified work to be read as a whole.[2] With this in mind, although we will break up Hosea into daily readings for our study, it may be helpful for you to read the whole book in one sitting before we dig into the text section by section.

POINT OF VIEW

Because Hosea's marriage symbolically mirrored God's relationship with and emotions toward His people, we will see that as Hosea prophesied, his point of view moved back and forth. Sometimes Hosea spoke *about God* in the third person. Other times he spoke in the first person *on behalf of God,* which is a relatively common feature of prophetic writings in Scripture. God gave His prophets a unique responsibility to speak divine revelations with His divine authority (Hebrews 1:1; Zechariah 7:12).[3]

PRONOUNS

Similar to how Hosea hops back and forth in point of view, the text also changes between masculine and feminine pronouns at different points. This does not indicate that Hosea was confused about God's distinction between male and female (Genesis 1:27) but is simply part of the poetic language of the book. In some chapters, Hosea likened Israel to a wife and spoke of the nation using the pronouns "*her*" and "*she*" (e.g., Hosea 2:2-4). In other places, Hosea referenced the tribe of Ephraim with the masculine pronoun "*he*" or with the plural pronoun "*they,*" meaning all the people (e.g., Hosea 4:17-19).

METONYMY

Hosea frequently employed this figure of speech that refers to one part or attribute of something to represent the larger whole. An example of metonymy is the phrase "the pen is mightier than the sword." Here, "the pen" refers to writing, and "the sword" refers to warfare and violence. For an example in Hosea, we can look at Hosea 12:11: *"If there is iniquity in Gilead, they shall surely come to nothing: in Gilgal they sacrifice bulls ..."* Hosea used the two cities of Gilead and Gilgal to represent the nation of Israel as a whole. This verse also points to two aspects of Israel's guilt: Gilead represented her social sins while Gilgal represented her idolatry.[4]

HELPFUL KEYWORDS *and* CONCEPTS *to* KNOW *in* HOSEA

> *Israel (aka Ephraim, Samaria, Jacob) — the nation God chose to be His people, rescued from slavery in Egypt, and led into the promised land (where they lived in Hosea's day before the Assyrian exile). In Hosea's time, "Israel" specifically referred to the northern tribe of the split kingdom.*

The word "Israel" is primarily included in this list to alert you to the synonyms Hosea will use throughout the book to refer to Israel. These include: Samaria, Ephraim and Jacob. When you read any of these words, Hosea is most likely referring to the northern kingdom of Israel as a whole. Samaria was the capital city of the northern kingdom. Ephraim was one of the strongest tribes of Israel and was likely still prominent in Hosea's time, and Jacob was a patriarch or forefather of God's people (whose name God changed to "Israel" in Genesis 32).

> *Syncretism — incorporating elements from other religions into one's faith and practice, resulting in a loss of integrity and assimilation to the surrounding culture.[1]*

While this word itself is not used anywhere in Hosea, syncretism was a prevailing sin among God's people throughout the book. In their minds, they may not have *rejected* God, but they thought they could continue to worship Him while also paying tribute to other gods. In reality, God's covenant with Israel required them to worship Him only and not to go after the gods of the nations that surrounded them (Deuteronomy 6:5-15). They were to love the Lord with all their hearts and serve Him with sincerity and faithfulness.

Second Kings 17:3-23 details the covenantal consequences of disobeying God's commands and practicing syncretism. It may be helpful to read this passage before studying Hosea.

> *Apostasy — spiritually turning away from God in rebellion or apathy, often in a permanent way, with no intention ever to turn back.*

Apostasy is presented by Hosea as infectious, spreading throughout the entire nation of Israel. Despite many warnings from prophets like Hosea, God's people refused to repent of their rebellion against Him, leading to their defeat and exile.[2]

> *Baal — a pagan fertility god who supposedly enabled the earth to produce crops and enabled people to produce children. The plural "Baals" can also refer to pagan deities in general.*

Baal cults challenged Israel's worship of God throughout their ancient history. Different cities and people groups in the Ancient Near East emphasized different attributes of Baal and developed special "denominations" of Baalism: Baal of Peor and Baal-berith are two examples (Numbers 25:3; Judges 8:33).[3] But all forms of Baal worship were false religions. In Hosea's time, every part of life in Israel — from work in the fields to beliefs about social duties to political decisions to relationships — was bound up with the worship of the Baals.

THEMES *of* HOSEA

WHILE the book of Hosea includes many themes, two of the most important have to do with love and knowledge. Hosea shows us a God who loves us and knows us, and our true calling is to know and love Him.

GOD'S LOVE

The love God demonstrates through the book of Hosea has been described in many ways:

- Steadfast.
- Consistent.
- Generous.
- Loyal.
- Sacrificial.
- Redemptive.
- Undying.
- Unconditional.

However, we will see a stark contrast between God's unconditional love and Israel's unreliable love. God's love for Israel was noble, unselfish, generous and protective. Israel's love was selfish, indulgent and pleasure-oriented (Hosea 2:4-17). Israel did not deserve God's love. But she received it anyways.[1]

Hosea displays the depth of God's love in both firmness and graciousness, expressed in both punitive and restorative ways. God did not withhold consequences for His people's sins; however, God also did not forget His promises to His people, and He proved that even when they did not love Him, He still loved them.

In Hosea's prophecies, God revealed His heart — a heart that is not cold, distant or robotic but is relational and involves a sense of emotion. While God's divine emotions are never uncontrolled or imperfect (like we know our own emotions can be), God does exhibit an emotional fervor He allows us to understand in human terms through books like Hosea.[2] God's love for the world that compelled Him to send Jesus as our Savior is the ultimate expression of His compassion (John 3:16) — and moments scattered throughout Hosea give us a glimpse into the heart of our loving God even in His lament of His people's unreliable love (Hosea 2:14-23; Hosea 6:4; Hosea 11:8-11).

GOD'S DESIRE FOR HIS PEOPLE
TO KNOW HIM

God's desire for His people to truly know Him is also a prominent theme in Hosea and is directly connected to their love — or lack of love — for Him (Hosea 4:6; Hosea 5:4; Hosea 6:3; Hosea 8:2; Hosea 11:3). *"No knowledge of God in the land"* was the cause of Israel's devastation (Hosea 4:1), but God's promise of redemption was *"you shall know the LORD"* (Hosea 2:20). At the core of Hosea's concern was the relationship between God and Israel. God alone was Israel's God, and they were God's chosen people. Hosea emphasized that true knowledge of God includes experiencing His loyal love.[3]

When speaking of this knowledge, Hosea often employed the Hebrew word *yada*. This word is used in a variety of ways in the Bible and can mean "to perceive, distinguish, acknowledge or know by experience."[4] The knowledge Hosea wrote about was characterized by a right relationship with God based on true faith, loyalty and obedience to Him. Sadly, Israel was pretending to know God (Hosea 6:3), but their rituals were empty.[5]

Today, we can have a right relationship with God through faith in Jesus, who is *"the radiance of the glory of God and the exact imprint of his nature"* (Hebrews 1:3). To *know* Christ is to *know* the one true God (John 17:3).

MAJOR MOMENTS

Week One

DAY ONE — HOSEA 1:1
Hosea introduced himself and the time of his writing.

DAY TWO — HOSEA 1:2-9
Hosea's marriage and the symbolic names of his children reflected Israel's coming judgment.

DAY THREE — HOSEA 1:10-11
Despite judgment, God promised Israel's future restoration and reunification.

DAY FOUR — HOSEA 2:1-6
Israel was rebuked for their unfaithfulness and warned of severe consequences.

DAY FIVE — HOSEA 2:7-13
Israel's pursuit of other gods was a futile search for satisfaction.

Week Two

DAY SIX — HOSEA 2:14-23
God promised to restore Israel and renew the covenant with His people.

DAY SEVEN — HOSEA 3:1-5
Hosea's love for his wife symbolized God's enduring love for Israel despite their unfaithfulness.

DAY EIGHT — HOSEA 4:1-6
God charged Israel with lacking faithfulness, love and knowledge of Him.

DAY NINE — HOSEA 4:7-14
The more Israel prospered, the more they sinned, and their leaders were justly condemned.

DAY TEN — HOSEA 4:15-19
Judah was warned not to follow Ephraim's idolatry.

Week Three

DAY ELEVEN — HOSEA 5:1-7
Priests and kings were rebuked for unfaithfulness.

DAY TWELVE — HOSEA 5:8-15
Israel wrongly sought rescue from Assyria instead of God.

DAY THIRTEEN — HOSEA 6:1-3
Hosea called for a return to the Lord, emphasizing God's mercy.

DAY FOURTEEN — HOSEA 6:4-11
Israel's attempts to seek the Lord with sacrifices were deemed insufficient.

DAY FIFTEEN — HOSEA 7:1-10
Israel's sins were exposed, including theft, deceit and arrogance.

Week Four

DAY SIXTEEN — HOSEA 7:11-16
Israelites cried out on their beds but said "no" to God in their hearts.

DAY SEVENTEEN — HOSEA 8:1-6
Israel once claimed to know God yet worshipped a golden calf.

DAY EIGHTEEN — HOSEA 8:7-14
Israel's reliance on foreign alliances was like sowing seed in the wind.

DAY NINETEEN — HOSEA 9:1-9
Israel saw prophets, channels of God's Word, as foolish.

DAY TWENTY — HOSEA 9:10-17
Israel's history of unfaithfulness led to God's expressions of anger.

Week Five

DAY TWENTY-ONE — HOSEA 10:1-8
Israel's luxuries led to increased idolatry.

DAY TWENTY-TWO — HOSEA 10:9-15
Among warnings of utter destruction, God pleaded for Israel to seek after Him.

DAY TWENTY-THREE — HOSEA 11:1-7
Despite God's love and care, Israel would make Assyria their king.

DAY TWENTY-FOUR — HOSEA 11:8-12
God's compassion tempered His judgment.

DAY TWENTY-FIVE — HOSEA 12:1-6
God recalled Israel's beginnings to remind the people He was their Helper.

Week Six

DAY TWENTY-SIX — HOSEA 12:7-14
God guided people through His prophets.

DAY TWENTY-SEVEN — HOSEA 13:1-8
Hosea demonstrated the absurdity of loving calves but hating people.

DAY TWENTY-EIGHT — HOSEA 13:9-16
God said He removed Israel's king in judgment, just as He had once put the king on the throne.

DAY TWENTY-NINE — HOSEA 14:1-7
Hosea called Israel to renounce their idols.

DAY THIRTY — HOSEA 14:8-9
God warned severely because He desired for His people to choose rightly and receive blessings.

WEEK ONE

Day 1 — HOSEA 1:1

Hosea introduced himself and the time of his writing.

———————————— ✤ ————————————

The first verse of Hosea sets the stage for what we will encounter throughout the entire book. In just one verse, Hosea introduced himself and his calling from God and gave context about the time in which he would faithfully speak the word of the Lord.

*Remember that at this point, the nation of Israel had divided into two kingdoms: Judah in the south and Israel in the north. Write the the names of the four **kings of Judah** listed in Hosea 1:1:*

*Who was the only **king of Israel** named in this list?*

"In the days of" these kings (v. 1), prosperity gave way to political upheaval and unrest for God's people. The economic prosperity in this era was rivaled only by the days of King David and King Solomon, who *"excelled all the kings of the earth in riches"* (2 Chronicles 9:22). Yet Hosea's time was also marked by spiritual sickness and confusion among God's people. Throughout the reigns of the kings listed in Hosea 1:1, Israel weakened, and the decaying nation attempted to find strength in every place but her loving God. The people worshipped foreign gods, trusted in their own resources, and sought political alliances with other nations like Egypt and Assyria.[1]

Hosea 1:1 focuses mainly on naming the kings of the southern kingdom, Judah, which is curious for a few reasons. While some of Hosea's prophecies included Judah (Hosea 6:4; Hosea 12:2), most were directed toward the northern kingdom of Israel. And as we said earlier in this study guide, Hosea himself likely lived and prophesied in Israel.

Historically, we also know that Israel during this period went through six kings, but scholars suggest Hosea listed only Jeroboam because he regarded Jeroboam as the last *legitimate king* of Israel. Perhaps Hosea was making a statement: Real kings follow the Lord.

Read the verses on the next page, recording how Jeroboam's successors came to power and what kind of "kings" they were.

KING	SCRIPTURES	DETAILS OF THE KING'S REIGN
Zechariah	2 KINGS 15:8-9	
Shallum	2 KINGS 15:10, 13, 15	
Menahem	2 KINGS 15:14, 16-20	
Pekahiah	2 KINGS 15:22-24	
Pekah	2 KINGS 15:25-28	
Hoshea	2 KINGS 15:30; 2 KINGS 17:1-6	

Following Jeroboam's rule, four of the next six kings of Israel were assassinated, and only three reigned for more than two years. The days following Jeroboam's reign were marked with anarchy, and Hosea likely believed none of the "kings" had a real right to the title. Some Bible scholars also suggest Hosea's focus on the kings of Judah in Hosea 1:1 revealed his hope that Judah would not follow Israel's downward spiral but would hear God's word of warning, repent, and move toward reunification with Israel.[2]

Hosea lived during a tumultuous time in an unsettled place among troubled people. Can you relate? How might this help you understand the book of Hosea?

As we begin our study of Hosea, we can acknowledge that while it was written at a specific time and place in history, the message of the book is not reserved only for that time and place. This book is part of our spiritual heritage; it was God's word to Israel, yes, but it also has applications for us today.[3]

"Heritage" can be defined as "a sense of identity passed down by generations." How would you describe your heritage (familial, national, cultural)? How has God's Word been part of your spiritual heritage?

In the same way our familial and cultural heritage shapes how we think and live, our spiritual heritage is a vital part of our past, present and future. As we lean into the ancient prophecies of Hosea, let's seek the Lord for what He desires to teach us about our own past so we may walk more freely and fully in His love today and in the future.

Day 2 — Hosea 1:2-9

Hosea's marriage and the symbolic names of his
children reflected Israel's coming judgment.

———— ❋ ————

Just two days into our study, we've already encountered a passage that doesn't feel very loving. But as we peel back the layers to discover what God was doing ... we will see His love in surprising ways.

In today's reading, God gave Hosea four commands, each followed by an explanation. The commands and explanations are connected by the word *"for."* Record them in the chart below:

	COMMAND	EXPLANATION (*"for ..."*)
HOSEA 1:2		
HOSEA 1:4		
HOSEA 1:6		
HOSEA 1:9		

As we've said, Hosea's marriage to Gomer was symbolic of God's relationship with His people — which is why it is so heartbreaking to see it described with words that painfully emphasize human unfaithfulness. The Hebrew word translated *"whoredom"* in the ESV Bible (Hosea 1:2) can also be translated as *"promiscuity"* (CSB), *"prostitution"* (AMP) or *"infidelity"* (NASB). Three times in verse 2, God used this word to describe:

1. The wife Hosea would marry.

2. The children Hosea would have with this wife.

3. The crimes of the land (God's people).

Scholars debate what exactly this descriptor was intended to communicate about Gomer, whether she made money as a prostitute or simply had a reputation for promiscuous behavior. Either way, the bottom line is sinful disloyalty — and God said *"the land"* was also connected to *"whoredom,"* reflecting the reality that all Israelites were guilty of sinful disloyalty to Him.

We know this was not an unfamiliar term to God's covenant people. Look up the verses below, and note how this word is used:

· *Exodus 34:15-16:*

· *Deuteronomy 31:16:*

God's people had forsaken Him (Hosea 1:2). Some translations say they were "*deserting*" (CEB) or "*abandoning*" (CSB) Him. They had not only turned **away** from God, but they had turned **against** Him — rejecting His unconditional love to worship other gods.

Hosea's marriage pointed to this prevailing problem: The people's relationship with God was broken and estranged. It is significant that God didn't just tell Hosea to have a casual or distant relationship but to enter into the covenant union of marriage with "*a **wife** of whoredom*" (Hosea 1:2, emphasis added). Hosea would experience the sorrows inflicted by an unfaithful wife much like God suffered the pains of covenant with unfaithful Israel. Hosea would bear in his human life an echo of the pain in God's heart for His people.

As believers in Jesus today, Scripture says we are His bride (Ephesians 5:31-32). Yet we, too, have been unfaithful (Romans 3:23). How does considering God as a faithful husband grieved by the unfaithfulness of His bride shape how you think about sin in your life?

Continuing in Hosea 1:4-9, we see each name of Hosea's children contained a message concerning God's coming judgment against Israel. "*Jezreel*" anticipated Israel's military defeat, "*No Mercy*" represented God's withdrawal of compassion and protection from His people, and "*Not My People*" culminated with the complete severance of the people from God.[1]

This last message-name, "*Not My People,*" would have taken the original hearers back to the days of Moses and the installation of God's covenant with Israel. The words "*I am*" in Hosea 1:9 recalled God's personal name — "*I AM WHO I AM*" — that He revealed to Moses as He promised to rescue His people from Egyptian slavery (Exodus 3:14).[2] But now God said "*I am **not** your God*" because in their disobedience, the people in Hosea's time were acting like they did not belong to Him (Hosea 1:9, emphasis added). Like there was no covenant. No accountability for their sin.

As we continue down this road with Hosea, we will learn more about how God's love for us is not disconnected from His punishment of sin — in fact, His punishment of sin is inseparable from His love. For today, let's dwell on the truth that although sin separates us from God, He has always had a plan to redeem.

Paul David Tripp brings God's love and justice into view as he writes about God's response to sin from the moment it entered the world in Genesis 3: "God took sin so seriously that he did two things when the first transgression occurred—he immediately meted out punishment and he immediately set in motion his plan of rescue and redemption."[3]

If we flip ahead in our Bibles, we see clearly that redemption comes through Jesus! What does 1 Peter 2:10 say to those who trust in Jesus, and how does this give you hope after today's reading in Hosea?

Day 3 — HOSEA 1:10-11

Despite judgment, God promised Israel's future restoration and reunification.

The first word of today's reading was likely a welcome word for the original hearers, and it is for us, too: "*Yet ...*" (Hosea 1:10).

This is similar to the phrase "*but God*" that signals divine intervention in dark situations throughout Scripture (Genesis 8:1; Genesis 50:20; Ephesians 2:3-5; etc.). With this conjunction in Hosea 1:10, God announced that though the immediate future of Israel would include judgment and destruction, that would not be the end of the story.

In referencing a people as numerous as the "*sand of the sea*" (v. 10), Hosea first looked back to Genesis, drawing on language from the long-ago covenant God made with Israel's patriarch Abraham: "*I will surely bless you, and I will surely multiply your offspring as the stars of heaven and as the sand that is on the seashore*" (Genesis 22:17). Then Hosea looked forward to a future day when the children of God would indeed be so great they "*cannot be measured or numbered*" (Hosea 1:10).

What did God say next in the second sentence of Hosea 1:10? How is this surprising after what we read in verse 9?

Although these verses might sound contradictory at first, this back-to-back punishment and promise actually reveal God's incredible mercy and love. It's like the Lord could hardly bear to hear Himself disown His people and sever ties with them in verse 9 — He followed up immediately in verse 10 with assurance that someday He would restore them and call them children again.

While this promised future was a welcome reversal of the imagery in verses 2-9, it also required faith. At the time Hosea uttered this prophecy, to imagine Israel becoming such a large nation would have been what one scholar calls "laughable."[1] The current state of Israel included an estimated 60,000 landowners and a total estimated population of 400,000 — paling in comparison to the size of Assyria, the superpower of the day and the nation that would soon ruin Israel.[2]

Describe a time when your circumstances appeared hopeless. Was it hard for you to have faith in God's love and promises? Why or why not?

God's promise of future restoration and reunification of Israel was nearly unforeseeable through human eyes ... which urged His people toward faith and hope in Him as "*the living God*" (v. 10). The phrase "*living God*" is one the original hearers of this prophecy likely would have connected to several other scriptures.

Look up the verses below, and record what they reveal about the "living God."

· *Deuteronomy 5:26:*

· *Joshua 3:10-13:*

· *Psalm 84:1-4:*

The false gods of foreign nations were dead or inanimate. Yet God's people called Him the "*living God,*" often in military contexts, identifying Him as active, true and victorious (e.g., 1 Samuel 17:26; 2 Kings 19:4).

Many years after Hosea prophesied, as the Apostle Paul preached the gospel of Jesus Christ, he also recalled Hosea 1:10 as a scripture that demonstrates how the living God treats His people "*with much patience*" despite our sins, ultimately "*to make known the riches of his glory*" (Romans 9:22-26). This was the hope of Israel in Hosea's day and is a hope we can cling to today. Through Jesus, God has made a way for us to become His children forever (John 1:12), and as children of God, **nothing** can separate us from His love (Romans 8:31-39).

What else do 2 Corinthians 6:16-7:1 and Romans 8:14-16 show us about being children of the living God?

As we embrace our position as children of the living God, let's allow Him to alert us to any changes we need to make to walk faithfully in His love. Let's allow our identity in Christ to shape our perspective on our current circumstances as well as our hope for the future.

Day 4 — Hosea 2:1-6

Israel was rebuked for their unfaithfulness and warned of severe consequences.

Hosea 2 opens with the same tone of hope and redemptive reversal that closed Chapter 1 — but then gives way to God's rebuke of Israel. This time, God started by calling Hosea to enlist brothers and sisters to plead to their mother for repentance (Hosea 2:1-2).

Scholars differ on who the brothers and sisters are in this text. Some propose these were Hosea's children as named in Chapter 1, or possibly they were children he adopted who were born to Gomer prior to her marriage to Hosea.[1] Others say the siblings represent a remnant of Israelites who remained faithful to the covenant with God.[2] There is no way to know with certainty who exactly was to do the pleading here; what is clear, however, is that the plea was directed toward the nation of Israel (the *mother* in this metaphor) as a whole.

The purpose of the plea was to move God's covenant people to repentance — turning away from their unfaithfulness and spiritual *adultery* with the Baals (Hosea 2:2). God exposed Israel's pursuit of other gods and her belief that false gods were to be praised for the provision of food, clothing and refreshment.

According to Hosea 2:5, what did Mother Israel say?

Look up the verses below, and compare the examples of God's provision to what Israel sought from false gods.

WHAT ISRAEL SOUGHT FROM *the* BAALS	GOD'S PROVISION
Bread	Exodus 16:14-15; John 6:35
Water	Exodus 15:24-26; John 4:10-14
Wool and flax (to make clothing)	Matthew 6:30-31
Drink (or wine)	Psalm 104:14-15; John 15:1
Oil	Psalm 23:5

Everything Israel prostituted herself to gain ... God was already giving her. Yet her pining for more provision, protection and prosperity led her to abandon the unmatched love and care of God.

> *In response to her persistence in going after other lovers, God promised to act. What two things does Hosea 2:6 say God would do? Why?*

God would give Israel the outcome she stubbornly pursued: separation from Him. Israel would lose her way as a nation, and Assyria would overtake her. Only then would she realize that the Baals were nowhere to be found and that they provided nothing in comparison to God, who controls the course of history.[3]

> *Generations before Hosea wrote that Israel "cannot find her paths" (v. 6), King Solomon recorded a much different image in Proverbs 3:5-6 and Proverbs 3:17. What do these verses say about paths? (Note that "she" in the latter proverb refers to wisdom.)*

These proverbs speak of safety and blessing that come with trusting in the Lord with all our hearts and acknowledging Him with all our ways. In this scenario, instead of being hedged in and held back (Hosea 2:6), the path of God's obedient children will be directed by His unconditional love and will lead to pleasantness and peace.

As we close today's study, let's ask God to show us where we've abandoned His paths to go after other things. Let's ask Him to reveal what we are tempted to lean on and look to instead of Him. Whatever He reveals, by His grace, we can be ready to repent and return to the Lord, our true love.

Day 5 — Hosea 2:7-13

Israel's pursuit of other gods was a futile search for satisfaction.

———————————— ✳ ————————————

The verses in today's reading continue to show Israel's resolute pursuit of other gods — and God's loving response to her stubborn ways. In some ways, God put a limit on Israel's wandering: He graciously said he would *"build a wall against her, so that she cannot find her paths,"* which were paths to her *"lovers"* or false gods (vv. 6-7). Still, Israel was responsible for the ways in which they *did* wander, and God would correct them for that.

Hosea 2:9-12 details six *"I will"* statements that declared God's course of action to correct His sinful people.

What are the six things God said He would do?

    1. Take back _____ *in its time (v. 9).*

    2. Take back _____ *in its season (v. 9).*

    3. Take away _____ *that covered nakedness (v. 9).*

    4. Uncover _____ *(v. 10).*

    5. Put an end to _____ *(v. 11).*

    6. Lay waste _____ *(v. 12).*

While giving herself to other gods and forgetting her one true God, Israel still observed the *"appointed feasts"* of covenant with the Lord (Hosea 2:11). Feast days, appointed by God Himself in His Word, were known as times of joy (Numbers 10:10) — but in spite of appearing to serve the Lord, Israel's heart was far from Him, and God would put an end to this hollow rejoicing.

Bible scholar Matthew Henry elaborates, "Sin and mirth can never hold long together; but if men will not take away sin from their mirth, God will take away mirth from their sin."[1]

    According to Hosea 2:8, what did Israel "not know"?

Today's passage contrasts Israel's view of her sin with God's view. One of the very feasts Israel likely continued to observe, the Feast of Firstfruits (Leviticus 23:9-14), was intended to remind God's people that *He alone* was their Provider — no one and nothing else but God Himself was the Giver of their crops. Yet Israel could not truly celebrate this festival when she did not know Him and did not acknowledge Him as her portion (Hosea 2:8). Instead, she attributed any prosperity and provision to her *"lovers"* (v. 12). God said this sin would be exposed as the depravity it was (v. 10).

It might feel easy to identify the error of ancient Israel's ways, but it's also important to see that the spiritual decay of Hosea's day is not all that different from our own. We might even find we have more in common with Israel's stubborn rebellion that we do with Hosea's righteous call for repentance.[2]

To address the realities of our own wayward hearts, let's consider two questions:

1. WHAT DO WE CELEBRATE THAT DOES NOT HONOR GOD?

Like the people of Hosea's day still observed feasts, we may engage in what appears to be joyful even while we actually grieve God's heart because our own hearts are far from Him.

Think about the things you celebrate and consider to be sources of joy. Is your joy coming from the Lord and honoring Him, or is there any "joy" that exalts earthly indulgences and selfish gain?

2. WHAT DO WE PRAISE FOR OUR PROVISION OTHER THAN GOD?

When we enjoy physical blessings like health or a good job, emotional blessings like strong community and vibrant relationships, or spiritual blessings like intimacy with God and enjoyment of His Word, we may attribute them to good luck. Or maybe we credit the favor of another person or our own hard work — but if so, we misunderstand where provision truly comes from. Certainly self-discipline and diligent work are important (Galatians 5:22-23; Proverbs 13:4). But we, like Israel, are to acknowledge God as the true source of everything we need.

Spend some time asking God to reveal the truth about who or what you believe to be the source(s) of provision in your life. Use the space below to record what God reveals:

List any words that come to mind about the abundance of God's provision — then look up those words in a Scripture concordance or a searchable online Bible, and write a few verses that show God's character as a Provider. Here are a few to get you started:

- · Provision — Philippians 4:19.   ·
- · Comfort — 2 Corinthians 1:3-5.   ·
- · Protection — 2 Samuel 22:2-4.   ·
- · Counsel — Isaiah 9:6.   ·

Week One
REFLECTION *and* PRAYER

In this first week of our study, we have come face to face with the wayward condition of God's people and the judgment that awaited them because of their spiritual stubbornness and blindness. And as we learned this week, the words recorded in Hosea are not only meant as a wake-up call for the generation of that day but also for us.

Yet even as we reflect on what we have in common with ancient Israel, we can also contrast their condition with the forever forgiveness that is possible today because of Jesus:

- Instead of shame (Hosea 2:10), in Christ, we have hope. "*Therefore since we have been justified by faith, we have peace with God through our Lord Jesus Christ. Through him we have also obtained access by faith into this grace in which we stand, and we rejoice in hope of the glory of God*" (Romans 5:1-2).

- Instead of chasing after other things (Hosea 2:5-7), in Christ, we can acknowledge God as our perfect portion (Psalm 119:57; 2 Peter 1:3).

Our study of Hosea will likely expose places of idolatry in our own lives, or areas where our devotion to other people, things or ideas is pulling us away from God. It's appropriate to grieve these sinful ways. But because of the grace of Jesus and His unconditional love, we can also rejoice that righteous grief and repentance will always lead us back to restored relationship with Him.

Let's pray.

Dear God, You are so good and gracious. Thank You for Your love that refuses to let us chase our own empty ways. Forgive us, Lord. Turn our eyes away from looking at worthless things, and give us life in Your ways. May our hearts be tender to Your call and quick to abandon our wicked ways. In Jesus' name, amen.

"i will betroth you to me forever.
i will betroth you to me
righteousness and in ju
steadfast love and in m
i will betroth you to me
and you shall know the Le
— Hosea 2:19-2

righteou
steadfas
l will be
faithful

275   From The D
Psalm 130. 8s and 7s.

1. From the depths do   I in-voke Thee,
2. Lord, if Thou shouldst mark transgressions
3. For   Je - ho - vah   I am wait-ing,
4. For   the Lord my   soul is wait-ing M

To my voice be Thou at-ten-tive
But with Thee there is for-give-ness, Th
In His word of   promise giv-en, Y
More than they for morning watching, W

CHORUS

Is - r'el hope thou in Je - ho - vah, Mercies great are found with Him;

NOTES

NOTES

NOTES

NOTES

WEEK TWO

Day 6 — Hosea 2:14-23

God promised to restore Israel and renew the covenant with His people.

———————— ✳ ————————

As today's reading begins, we find more prophecies about Israel in the wilderness. Up to this point in the history of God's people, the wilderness had often been connected to punishment. But this prophecy, somewhat surprisingly, goes in a different direction.

According to Hosea 2:14, who would lead Israel to the wilderness? (Hint: The speaker in this passage is named in verses 16 and 21.)

What three things would God do in the wilderness (vv. 14-15)?

· *Speak* _____ .

· *Give* _____ .

· *Make* _____ .

What would Israel do in response (v. 15)?

Israel would walk in the wilderness, but she would not be alone. God would not abandon His bride. With this in mind, Hosea looked back in history and then looked forward as he prophesied a great reversal from shame to salvation for God's people.

First, Hosea looked back. The wilderness he described in Hosea 2:14 called to mind the Israelites' exodus from slavery in Egypt about 700 years earlier, when *"God led the people around by the way of the wilderness"* (Exodus 13:18), and *"the LORD commanded Moses on Mount Sinai ... in the wilderness of Sinai"* (Leviticus 7:38). It was in this first wilderness that God revealed Himself to His people and gave them His promises (Exodus 6:6-8). He showed them His love and taught them His ways.

In Hosea's time, when God's people refused to acknowledge Him in their land, God promised to lead them back to where they first realized His love and care for them. In that wilderness place, He would *"speak tenderly to"* Israel (Hosea 2:14). The Hebrew wording of this phrase can also be translated as "speak to her heart."

To speak to someone's heart requires knowledge of and concern for them. The hearts of God's people needed healing, correction, understanding ... and love. Only God's unconditional love could meet His people where they were, lead them out of their bondage (even when they didn't recognize it as bondage), and heal them in the wilderness.

What is your response to the reality that God knows your heart and is concerned about your spiritual and emotional state?

The wilderness that once referred to destruction and exile, called "*a parched land*" in Hosea 2:3, would now represent hope and restoration. And today's reading also contains a number of other redemptive reversals:

- The vineyards that were ruined (Hosea 2:12) would be restored (v. 15).
- The Valley of Achor (which means "trouble" in Hebrew) would become a door of hope (v. 15).
- The animals that once devoured the land (Hosea 2:12) would live in peace with the people (v. 18).
- The bow and the sword that once slaughtered (Hosea 1:4-5) would be abolished or broken (Hosea 2:18).
- The nation that once forgot her God (Hosea 2:13) would forget the Baals (v. 17).
- The bride who once did not know Him (Hosea 2:8) would "*know the LORD*" (v. 20) and call Him "*My Husband*" (v. 16).

The reversals come full circle with the names of Hosea's children. Let's compare what was said of the children in Chapter 1 with what we read in today's verses.

	HOSEA 1	HOSEA 2
Jezreel		
No Mercy		
Not My People		

Tucked into today's reversals is the hope of a new future covenant — a new betrothal between God and His people, sealed with His righteousness, justice, steadfast love, mercy and faithfulness (Hosea 2:19-20).

Today we see the fulfillment of this new covenant in Jesus Christ. God's love and faithfulness not only restored and renewed His relationship with Israel, but God has made a way for *all who will believe* to come to Him. He has sent us His Son. Because He loved us first, we are able to love Him (1 John 4:19). Even if it feels like you're in a wilderness today, allow God to speak this gospel Truth tenderly to your heart and draw you nearer to Him.

The Wilderness in Scripture

Throughout the Bible, the wilderness depicts a place — although often a spiritually, emotionally and physically difficult place — of encountering God.

GOD PROVIDES FOR HIS PEOPLE IN THE WILDERNESS. The wilderness requires God's people to rely on Him alone. For instance, God fed Israel with manna, or bread from heaven, in the wilderness on their journey from slavery in Egypt to freedom in the promised land (Exodus 16:11-16). And manna wasn't the only thing He provided: His provision was so complete that not even their shoes wore out on the long journey (Deuteronomy 29:5). In the New Testament, Jesus also fed thousands of people in *"a desolate place,"* providing enough food for everyone to eat until they were satisfied (Matthew 15:32-38).

GOD PROTECTS HIS PEOPLE IN THE WILDERNESS. God ensured that David, whom He chose to be king of Israel, found sanctuary in the wilderness though his enemies pursued him (1 Samuel 23:14). Later David even longed for the wilderness and the security and relief he felt there (Psalm 55:6-8).

GOD PREPARES HIS PEOPLE IN THE WILDERNESS. The wilderness is sometimes a training ground that leads God's people into their purpose. It can represent a place of spiritual testing, repentance and growth. Deuteronomy 8:2 says God led Israel in the wilderness for 40 years to test their hearts. Centuries later, John the Baptist preached repentance in the wilderness (Matthew 3:1-3), and Jesus Himself was tempted by Satan in the wilderness — where He triumphed over the enemy! — as the final act of preparation for His ministry on earth (Matthew 4).

In much the same way ancient people of God experienced Him in the wilderness, we can experience Him today. Whether it is the wilderness of desolate circumstances or a season that feels spiritually dry, we can look for and count on God's provision, protection and preparation to meet us there.[1]

Day 7 — HOSEA 3

Hosea's love for his wife symbolized God's enduring
love for Israel despite their unfaithfulness.

Chapter 3 begins with a new command from God to Hosea: *"Go again, love a woman who is loved by another man and is an adulteress, even as the* Lord *loves the children of Israel, though they turn to other gods"* (Hosea 3:1). There is debate about whether or not this woman was Gomer or whether Gomer had left Hosea, causing a divorce, and God meant for Hosea to enter into a second marriage with another woman. For the purposes of our study, let's look at two keywords that point to Gomer:

The first keyword is *"woman."* Given how Hosea 1 emphasizes the *names* of his family members, if Hosea 3:1 meant Hosea would marry another woman besides Gomer, it would have been consistent for Hosea to name and describe her in more detail.[1]

The second keyword is *"adulteress."* To be an adulteress would require the woman to be married, then unfaithful to the marriage. For Hosea to love another adulteress other than his own wife would raise additional questions about the morality of his actions, but this is not the point of the book of Hosea. The focus is on God's love for Israel despite her unfaithfulness. For these reasons and others, it seems likely this was Gomer, Hosea's unfaithful wife, whom he set out to redeem from bondage.

According to Hosea 3:2, what did Hosea do in obedience to God's instruction?

The fact that Hosea had to buy his wife implies she had fallen into some form of slavery.[2] The combining of both silver and barley for payment also suggests Hosea did not have enough money to pay the price to buy back his wife, but he was willing to do whatever it took. Further, the Hebrew verb translated *"bought"* (v. 2) includes the idea of haggling.[3] The scene depicts Hosea persistently and intensely offering everything he had, even to the point of humiliation, for the sake of redeeming his wife. To love his adulterous wife — again — required payment from Hosea, and it also required humility.

Describe a time when you felt rejected and abandoned by someone you love. After the actions that hurt you so much, how would you feel about sacrificing for the sake of the person who caused you to feel that way?

Why do you think God called Hosea to show humility in this way, and how does this mirror His love for us?

In spite of her willful rejection, Hosea gave **everything** to rescue his wife from bondage and bring her back into a loving relationship with himself. Hosea's actions illuminated God's love for Israel in spite of her rejection of Him — and also pointed forward to God's greatest sacrificial act of love.

God loved us so much He sent Jesus to pay the ultimate price for our sin: He died for us while we were yet sinners (Romans 5:8). Jesus was spit on and beaten. His clothes were stripped off, and He was mocked and insulted. He was not guilty, yet He bore the guilt and shame meant for us (Isaiah 53:6). He humbled Himself even to the point of death on a cross (Philippians 2:8). Jesus endured the shame of the cross, though He scorned it, so that His resurrection could pave the way from shame to glory for all who believe in Him (Hebrews 12:2-3).

Ultimately *this* was God's act of love toward Israel that would one day bring her back into restored relationship with Him, so the people could *"return and seek the LORD their God ... come in fear to the LORD and to his goodness in the latter days"* (Hosea 3:5). When we trust Jesus as Lord and Savior, we receive His goodness and look forward to the crown of glory that awaits us in eternity (1 Peter 5:4).

In our fast-paced society, we can so easily rush past the reality of the gospel. Today, let's slow our pace long enough to sit with this expression of God's unfathomable love.

*There are likely things going on in your life right now that make you feel worried, angry, discouraged or possibly even hopeless. How does God's love, demonstrated through Jesus giving **everything** to save you, change how you view what you're facing today?*

In light of God's love, what actions or attitudes might you need to turn from in order to "seek the LORD ... come in fear to the LORD and to his goodness" (Hosea 3:5)?

As we close today, if you're able, listen to a worship song, and offer a sacrifice of praise to Him.

Day 8 — Hosea 4:1-6

God charged Israel with lacking faithfulness, love and knowledge of Him.

⁂

The call to Israel that begins Chapter 4 indicates a division in the book of Hosea. No longer would Hosea chronicle his personal life and marriage; instead, his remaining prophecies focus on Israel directly.

Chapter 4 opens with the tone of a formal indictment, like in a courtroom, with the Lord bringing charges against Israel. The first two verses lay out His charges in two lists: things that *were* in Israel and things that *were not*.

Below, record the words that follow "there is no" *and* "there is" *in Hosea 4:1-2.*

THERE IS NO ...   THERE IS ...

The mention of swearing, lying, murdering, stealing and committing adultery (Hosea 4:2) recalls the Ten Commandments God had given to Israel through Moses in the wilderness. In Exodus 20:13-15, murder, stealing and adultery are specifically outlawed by God. Lying is forbidden in the ninth commandment, *"You shall not bear false witness against your neighbor"* (Exodus 20:16), as is swearing in the third commandment, *"You shall not take the name of the LORD your God in vain"* (Exodus 20:7).

And these actions were directly connected to what was *not* in the land, according to Hosea 4:1: There was no knowledge of God, steadfast love or faithfulness. In the introduction of our study, we discussed Israel's knowledge of God — or rather, how they *"rejected knowledge"* (v. 6). The idea of *"steadfast love"* (v. 1) points to a love that goes beyond the mere obligations of a relationship and freely gives kindness to another. But for today, let's spend some time on the quality of **faithfulness.**

"Faithfulness" has been defined as "the wholesomeness of soul that comes from a life that follows principle." Faithfulness therefore requires both steadfast love and knowledge of God. As the Bible tells us, God is love (1 John 4:8), so steadfast love is directly connected to the knowledge of God and His principles. Faithfulness can also be summarized as "a determination to know the truth and live by it."[1]

What are some things you are determined *to do at home, work, or other areas of your life? What is the evidence of your determination? (For instance: putting those things on your calendar, spending money or time on them, etc.)*

What evidence in your life shows faithful determination to know God's Truth and live by it? How could you strengthen your spiritual determination?

During the days Hosea prophesied, the nation of Israel was no longer determined to know God's Truth and live by it. They had set their hearts toward other things, and because of that, the people and even the land and animals of Israel would face ruin and destruction (Hosea 4:3-6).

In today's world, we, too, face worldly distractions and temptations that contend for our attention and our devotion. The book of Hebrews warns Christians to *"pay much closer attention"* to the Word of God so we will not *"drift away from it"* (Hebrews 2:1). Like Israel, we must recognize that our pursuit of Christ, His ways, and the abundant life that comes from following Him cannot be passive. We must choose to pursue Him daily so we may know the Truth and live by it.

What do you need to say "no" to in order to be faithful to God today? What do you need to say "yes" to?

Day 9 — Hosea 4:7-14

The more Israel prospered, the more they sinned, and their leaders
were justly condemned.

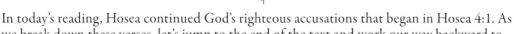

In today's reading, Hosea continued God's righteous accusations that began in Hosea 4:1. As we break down these verses, let's jump to the end of the text and work our way backward to trace how the conclusion of today's reading shows the logical yet devastating outcome of sin.

What does Hosea 4:14 say "a people without understanding shall come to" *in the end?*

The final word of this verse also appears in Proverbs 10:10 and Proverbs 10:8. How do all three verses share a similar message?

The lack of understanding that would ruin the nation of Israel is described in more detail in Hosea 4:10-12. Let's look closer at two important descriptors:

1. *"They have forsaken the LORD to cherish whoredom, wine, and new wine, which take away the understanding"* (vv. 10-11).
2. *"A spirit of whoredom has led them astray"* (v. 12).

Here "*whoredom*" refers to the spiritual adultery of the nation, and "*understanding*" describes the people's hearts and minds, including their character, strength of will and ability to reason.[1] Verse 11 points to the fact that like delighting in too much wine can dull the mind and the senses, delighting in sin and idolatry can too.[2]

The Israelites likely would not have described themselves as "delighting in sin and idolatry" — but this was actually evidence of how dull they'd become. Verses 11-12 depict a person whose mind can no longer recognize the error of their ways or their wanderings as they go "*astray*." This kind of dullness requires something like the shriek of a siren to shake the mind from its stupor — which is part of God's intention in the book of Hosea, both for Israel and for us.

Spend some time asking God to reveal any places in your mind that have been dulled to sin and idolatry. Use the space below to record what the Holy Spirit brings up in your heart:

Read Ephesians 5:15-20. Instead of walking foolishly with minds dulled by sin and idolatry, who fills us as believers in Jesus, and how do we respond?

Now let's get back to Hosea 4:12 and the phrase *"a spirit of whoredom has led them astray."* In Hebrew, the word for "led astray" carried the idea of "getting out from under," so here we see an ironic twist on the way God *"brought [Israel] out from under the burdens of the Egyptians"* (Exodus 6:7).[3] God's people were now trying to get "out from under" **Him**, the very One who freed them!

Read the following passages, and record what they reveal about Israel trying to get out from under God's authority and covenant.

· *Exodus 14:10-12:*

· *Exodus 32:1-8:*

· *Numbers 14:1-4:*

Our culture may tell us to trust our instincts and let our hearts be our compass for what we should or should not do. The Bible, however, makes it clear that our hearts, like Israel's, are prone to wander. In the middle of a prophecy about Jesus, the prophet Isaiah confirmed, *"All we like sheep have gone astray; we have turned—every one—to his own way"* (Isaiah 53:6).

We need spiritual leadership and direction. We need a shepherd. And sadly, Hosea 4:7-9 tells us Israel's spiritual leaders (priests) were corrupt and selfish ... but today we know God has given us a Good Shepherd. Not only does Jesus lead us and guide us, but He took the punishment and judgment for sin that belonged to us (John 10:11-18).

Let us determine today to linger in our Shepherd's presence and allow Him to wake us entirely from any spiritual stupor in our hearts.

Use the space below to offer a prayer of repentance for any ways you've wandered, and thank Jesus for His unconditional love that makes a way for us to return to Him.

DAY 10 — HOSEA 4:15-19

Judah was warned not to follow Ephraim's idolatry.

❋

As we close Week 2 of our study, we have seen that God in His love warned Israel (Hosea 4:5-6). He pleaded with them (Hosea 2:2). He promised restoration and redemption if they returned to Him (Hosea 2:21-23). He alerted them of the ruin that awaited if they continued on their current path (Hosea 2:10-13).

Yet Israel would not hear or respond.

How did Hosea describe the people in Hosea 4:16?

Because of their stubbornness, what did God tell Judah to do with Israel — also called Ephraim — in verses 15 and 17?

In verse 15, the command to *"enter not into Gilgal, nor go up to Beth-aven"* referenced sacred sites steeped in spiritual history for Israel:

GILGAL

- · Israel camped at Gilgal after God miraculously made a way for them to cross the Jordan River into the promised land (Joshua 4:19).
- · At Gilgal, the men of Israel were circumcised (a sign of God's covenant) in preparation for the nation's first Passover (commemorating God's deliverance) in the promised land (Joshua 5:7-12).
- · Israel crowned its first king, Saul, in Gilgal (1 Samuel 11:14-15).
- · King David was welcomed home from battle at Gilgal (2 Samuel 19:15).

· In Hebrew, *beth-aven* means "city of wickedness," and *bethel* means the "city of God." Geographically, Beth-aven and Bethel were two actual cities near one another (see Joshua 7:2), but in Hosea 4:15, the prophet used "Beth-aven" as a derogatory way to refer to Bethel as a fallen city. Hosea used a pun to make a point about the irony of the wickedness in the city of God.

· Abraham camped at Bethel and built an altar there (Genesis 12:8).

· God gave Jacob a vision of a stairway to heaven at Bethel (Genesis 28:11-19) and called Himself the *"God of Bethel"* (Genesis 31:13).

As the nation became rebellious, these sites were *"joined to idols"* (Hosea 4:17) and became centers for apostasy (remember this term from our keyword list on Page 13?). God instructed the people of Judah not to go near such places and went as far as to say *"leave [Ephraim] alone"* (v. 17).

Finally, there is some debate over translations of verse 16, but scholars mostly agree the image of *"a lamb in a broad pasture"* depicts an animal alone in the countryside, perhaps resisting or fleeing from the shepherd who would guard and guide it.[1]

To better understand this, let's read Psalm 81:8-16 and answer the questions below.

· What were God's instructions in Psalm 81:9?

· What did God, the Good Shepherd, remind His people in Psalm 81:10?

· In Psalm 81:13-16, what did God say His people would gain if they would listen to Him?

Many scholars place the writing of this psalm around the same time Hosea prophesied. Here again we find God imploring His children to listen to Him and return — yet because they refused, God's justice compelled Him to give them over to their stubborn hearts (Psalm 81:12).

In the New Testament, Paul wrote about a similar heart condition. Following the resurrection of Jesus, Paul described how people of his day *"knew God"* but *"did not honor him as God or give thanks to him, but they became futile in their thinking, and their foolish hearts were darkened ... they exchanged the truth about God for a lie and worshiped and served the creature rather than the Creator"* (Romans 1:21-25). For this reason, God *"gave them up"* to their sins (Romans 1:24; Romans 1:26).

It's important to see that even when God gives us up to experience the consequences of our sin, He is not giving up on us altogether, as though to say, *Well, I guess this one is just impossible for Me to save. Too bad!* Rather, God allows us to see what it's like to walk away from Him precisely because *He wants us to come back,* trust in Him and dwell with Him forever.

> *What does 2 Peter 3:9 say about who God wants to save? How might God's discipline help us "reach repentance"?*

In His love, God pursues us. Every day of our lives, He offers us redemption by grace through faith in His Son, Jesus. At the same time, in His love, God does not force His people to follow Him. He gave Israel a choice to receive His love and follow His ways, and He gives us the same choice today.

As we've seen in Hosea, we can refuse God — but if we do, we will only find grief, shame and pain as the result (Hosea 4:19). Instead, friend, let's choose Him. Let's not go one more day ignoring His love or assuming His love will ignore our sinful compromises. Let's commit anew today to honor God and give thanks to Him.

Week Two

REFLECTION *and* PRAYER

Twice this week, we read that God's people **forgot** Him — and it led to pain and chaos in their lives (Hosea 2:13; Hosea 4:6). Yet God reminded His people of His faithfulness in the past as He entreated them to listen to Him and trust Him in the present, which would lead to blessing and peace. To remain in the care of God's unconditional love today, we, too, can practice remembering how He's *already* demonstrated His love both to us personally and to people throughout history.

As we continue reading about the depths of the stubborn, sinful choices of God's people, the depths of God's unconditional love become more and more astounding. How could He keep loving a people so bent on rejecting Him? Yet He did — and He does. Israel's sin long ago is no different than our sin today in that both their sins and ours demand God's justice. But Jesus has paid the price. For all who believe in Him, no sin is too great for His blood to forgive.

Let's pray.

Thank You, God, for Your love. Thank You for this week's study that has been deeply convicting and relieving all at the same time. I'm grieved by my sin and my stubbornness to continue in it. But I'm freed by Your grace and the truth that You love me and will never stop loving me. By the power of the Holy Spirit, make me more like You. I want to learn to walk in Your ways and honor You with my life. In Jesus' name, amen.

"i will betroth you to me forever.
i will betroth you to me ...
righteousness and in jus...
steadfast love and in m...
i will betroth you to me ...
and you shall know the L...
— Hosea 2:19-2...

275   From The D...

Psalm 130. 8s and 7s.

1. From the depths do I in-voke Thee,
2. Lord, if Thou shouldst mark transgressions
3. For Je - ho - vah I am wait-ing,
4. For the Lord my soul is wait-ing M...

To my voice be Thou at-ten-tive A...
But with Thee there is for-give-ness, Th...
In His word of promise giv-en, Y...
More than they for morning watching, W...

CHORUS

Is - r'el hope thou in Je - ho - vah, Mercies great are found with Him;

righteou...
steadfas...
l will be...
faithful...

NOTES

NOTES

NOTES

NOTES

WEEK THREE

Day 11 — HOSEA 5:1-7

Priests and kings were rebuked for unfaithfulness.

———————————— ✳ ————————————

The opening exclamations of Hosea 5:1 progress like the resounding claps of a cymbal: *"Hear this ... Pay attention ... Give ear, O house of the king!"* The repeated calls were meant to demand the attention of the prophet's audience. However, the words that followed would not have been what they wanted to hear. Today's reading opens with a verdict of judgment for the charges God brought against Israel in Chapter 4.

Who in particular was the judgment for, according to Hosea 5:1?

The final words of verse 1 list two religious sites the people in Hosea's day would have recognized: Mizpah and Mount Tabor. *"A snare at Mizpah and a net spread upon Tabor"* described these once-sacred places of worship as a type of trap where people were now incited to worship idols.

What did God's people do at Mizpah in 1 Samuel 7:5-6? How is this different from what they were doing in Hosea 5?

Next, scholars differ on their translations of Hosea 5:2. The ESV says, *"revolters have gone deep into slaughter"* (Hosea 5:2), but others render the phrase *"dug a deep pit to trap them at Acacia Grove"* (NLT) or use similar language about a pit.[1] There is no way to know for sure which image was Hosea's exact intention, but both *"deep into slaughter"* and *"pit to trap them"* convey the same message: Israel's spiritual leaders, political leaders, and the nation as a whole were deep in sin ... and God saw it all.

After pronouncing the reason for His judgment, God revealed His knowledge of all the people's deeds: *"I know Ephraim, and Israel is not hidden from me"* (Hosea 5:3).

Read Genesis 3:6-10. What happened to Adam and Eve after they ate fruit from the tree God instructed them not to eat from (v. 7)?

What did they feel and do when their eyes were opened?

It's an ancient truth: Humans attempt to get away with sin. We listen to the enemy of our Savior and of our souls, and the enemy deceives us (Genesis 3:13). Our own desires also lure and entice us (James 1:14). Then when we do what is wrong, we often make futile attempts to hide our sin and ourselves from God.

But this didn't work for Adam and Eve. It didn't work for the Israelites of Hosea's day. And it won't work for us today. **God knows.**

It's interesting how that statement can go two ways:

1. Sometimes we deeply *want God to know*. We want Him to know our needs, acknowledge our desires and understand our pain.
2. Other times we *don't want God to know*. We want Him to dismiss our disobedience, turn His eyes away when we compromise His commands, and overlook our selfish indulgences.

What situations, emotions, hopes or struggles have you openly brought to the Lord and desired for Him to know and acknowledge? How can you rejoice that He does indeed see these things?

What are you inclined to try to cover up and hide from God? How can you honestly confess these things to Him, knowing He already sees all?

God is not a God who knows only sometimes. He knows all the time, and nothing is hidden from Him. Commentator Matthew Henry says this of the nation of Israel: "The piercing eye of God saw secret liking and disposition to sin, the love the house of Israel had for their sins, and the dominion their sins had over them."[2] God saw their disposition to sin then, and He sees ours now.

Although we have all loved sin ... God loves us.

He loves us too much *not* to call us away from brokenness and toward healing and repentance. So today, let's stop dismissing or covering up the reality of the sickness of our sin. Instead, let's bring our whole hearts to God and receive His healing grace, trusting in His unconditional love to forgive us and create clean hearts in us (Psalm 51:10).

MAP *of* ISRAEL DURING HOSEA'S TIME

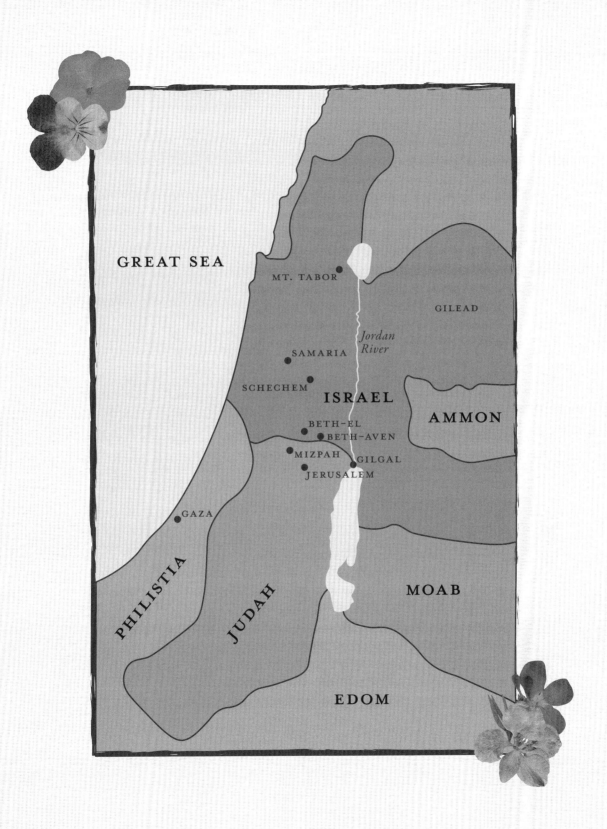

Day 12 — Hosea 5:8-15

Israel wrongly sought rescue from Assyria instead of God.

— ❋ —

A command to *"sound the alarm"* begins today's reading — Hosea 5:8 conveys the idea of multiple watchmen, soldiers on the lookout for an approaching enemy, blowing horns to warn of impending danger.

The danger in this case could have been the Assyrian army that would eventually conquer Israel and lead them into exile. But whether through the Assyrians or some other foe, today's text makes clear who Israel would *truly* be fighting against: God Himself (Hosea 5:10; Hosea 5:12-14).

What three things did God describe Himself as being "like" *in Hosea 5:12 and verse 14?*

1.

2.

3.

These images are vivid and their message inescapable: God had become like an agent of decay and destruction to Israel.

Scholar Duane Garrett makes the interesting observation that the images of decay (moths and rot) indicate a sustained demise over time while a lion represents a sudden, violent end.[1] For years, God had warned Israel and urged her to return to Him. But for years, she had ignored His pleas, leaving her nation in a state of gradual decay. Now she would also face sudden destruction from an enemy invasion.

Yesterday we read that God *"ha[d] withdrawn"* from Israel (Hosea 5:6), and the final verse of today's reading similarly pictures God as a lion who would return to His place until Israel acknowledged their guilt and sought Him (Hosea 5:15).

For all of us, there will come a time when if we have chosen to reject God's love, we will face His wrath (Hosea 5:10). God graciously offers us new mercies every morning of our lives (Lamentations 3:22-23), but at some point, we will all see our last morning on earth.

Read the verses below, and write down what you learn about when *and how long* we are able to seek the Lord.

· *Isaiah 55:6:*

· *John 12:36a:*

· *Psalm 32:6:*

From the patriarchs to the prophets to the words of Jesus Himself, we find the Bible entreating us to seek, believe and pray *while the Lord may be found.* We learn two things from this:

1. TODAY THE LORD MAY BE FOUND. Today is a gift from the Lord. Today we can seek the Lord, believe in Him and pray. Today we can repent, receive His love, and be restored to a perfect relationship with Him through faith in Christ! We can exhort each other not to be hardened by sin's deceitfulness "*as long as it is called 'today'*" (Hebrews 3:13). We can spur one another on to love and good deeds. Today we can meet together and encourage one another (Hebrews 10:24-25).

2. THERE WILL BE A DAY WHEN THE LORD CAN'T BE FOUND BY THOSE WHO HAVE NOT REPENTED. What a despairing day that will be for those who don't trust in Jesus. As the Israelites experienced the retreat of their God and a "*day of punishment*" (Hosea 5:9) because of their sinful choices, let us learn from them. Let's not put off repentance and obedience until tomorrow when we can have faith today (James 4:14). Let's not boast about tomorrow and the plans we have made for ourselves (Proverbs 27:1). Let's be wise and watchful today so we will be prepared for the Lord's return (Matthew 25:1-13).

What might you do differently today when you remember that the Lord may still be found? How does this give you hope as well as a sense of urgency to share the gospel with people who haven't found Jesus yet?

Before the Israelites entered the promised land, God warned them not to forget Him and foretold that punishment would await them if they did. But He also promised that even in the place of exile, "*You will seek the LORD your God and you will find him, if you search after him with all your heart and with all your soul*" (Deuteronomy 4:29).

Are you seeking the Lord with all your heart and soul? If there's anything you're withholding, how could you surrender and seek the Lord with your whole heart today?

With one word, today's reading in Hosea closes with a reminder of hope: "*I will return again to my place, **until** they acknowledge their guilt and seek my face ...*" (Hosea 5:15, emphasis added). God had withdrawn from Israel, but He hadn't withdrawn forever. When we confess our sins, God is faithful and just to forgive us, cleanse us from all unrighteousness, and draw near to us once again (1 John 1:9; James 4:8).

DAY 13 — HOSEA 6:1-3

Hosea called for a return to the Lord.

As is often the case in the book of Hosea, in the midst of doom and gloom, we encounter a ray of hope. In the first three verses of Chapter 6, Hosea encouraged God's people that there was still time for them to respond positively to the final warnings of Chapter 5. Hosea called, *"Come, let us return to the LORD"* (Hosea 6:1).

Why did Hosea say they should return to the Lord? What could they expect to happen when they returned (Hosea 6:1-3)?

Though God was the One who *"struck [Israel] down"* (v. 1), He promised that when they called to Him from their place of despair, He would answer and *"raise [them] up"* (v. 2). Though they would experience punishment for breaking their covenant with God, He would faithfully heal them and tenderly bind their wounds. (See also Job 5:18 and 2 Chronicles 7:14.)

Even God striking down Israel was a mercy designed to awaken their hearts to repentance. In fact, this mercy and awakening can only come *from God*, which is why Scripture speaks of God Himself granting repentance (2 Timothy 2:25; Acts 5:31; Acts 11:18). Sin leaves us spiritually dead, unable to turn to God on our own (Ephesians 2:1; 1 Corinthians 2:14; Romans 8:7-8). So God gets all the glory even for our repentance! At the same time, when we repent willingly *because* He has changed our hearts, God rewards us with even more grace. As scholar Thomas McComiskey so beautifully states, "It is a universal truth that when a spiritually dead people turn in humility to God, he will respond in mercy."[1]

Hosea 6:2 presents the image of a person on a sickbed being restored to health — or indeed, a dead person being *"revive[d]"* — which looked forward to the day when Israel would be reestablished as a nation and restored to her original state of stability and strength.[2]

According to verse 2, the Lord would raise up His people for them to do what? (Hint: It follows the word "that.")

The language in verse 2 anticipated God's quick response to the genuine repentance of His people. It would only be a short time before God raised up Israel so His people could live abundantly in His presence.

Hosea 6:2 says God would raise the dead to life "on the third day." This didn't mean literally 72 hours, but it did mean death would not last forever. How might this also relate to the "dawn" imagery in verse 3?

As we've seen before in Hosea, God wanted His people to **know Him.** The kind of knowing Hosea described when he said *"let us press on to know the Lord"* (Hosea 6:3) is not a casual, distant knowing. It means to know God intimately and personally. The Hebrew word is *yada*. This is the same word used in Genesis to describe the kind of relationship Adam and Eve had when they conceived a child: *"Adam **knew** Eve his wife"* (Genesis 4:1, emphasis added).

Furthermore, the phrase *"let us press on"* in Hosea 6:3 could also be translated "let us pursue." This sets the knowledge of God as an object of fervent pursuit for His people.[3] Hosea called God's people to chase after Him with untiring resolve so they could remember His commands, learn His ways, and follow Him no matter what. The CSB translation says, *"Let's strive to know the Lord"* (v. 3).

What do you strive for in your family, career, community, relationships or other areas of life? What would it look like for you to strive to know the Lord?

To strive for knowledge of God requires us to cease striving after other things; as we've learned from Israel, going after other things will never satisfy our souls. Today let's choose to stop chasing after earthly balms we believe will comfort or fulfill us, and let's instead offer all our energies to the only worthy pursuit: knowing our Savior more. Let's resolve ahead of time that we will not grow weary or lose heart in our pursuit of Jesus.

Hosea 6:3 says God "will come to us as the showers, as the spring rains that water the earth." How does Jesus come to us, according to John 4:14? What does this tell us about God's unconditional love?

Day 14 — HOSEA 6:4-11

Israel's attempts to seek the Lord with sacrifices were deemed insufficient.

———————————— ✳ ————————————

In Hosea 4:15, it appeared the southern kingdom of Judah was not yet guilty of the same offenses as the northern kingdom of Israel; however, our reading today opens with God's lament over both Israel and Judah. Hosea now displayed Israel and Judah as two equals in their hollow devotion to God.

How did God describe Israel and Judah's love for Him in Hosea 6:4? How does this contrast with what we learned about God's love in Hosea 6:3?

While God loved faithfully and unconditionally, the love of His people came and went like the morning dew. The difference was so despairing that God asked — twice — *"What shall I do with you"* (v. 4)? Scholars suggest we can see God's frustration with His people's inconsistent love, constant wavering and outright apostasy in the sudden and puzzling shifts in the text throughout the book of Hosea.[1]

In verse 6, what did God clearly state as His desire for His people?
"For I desire _____ _____ and not_____ ,
the _____ of _____ rather than_____ _____ ."

Animal sacrifices were instituted by God in the Old Testament to demonstrate the severity of sin and show that sin requires justice (Hebrews 9:22). However, what God desired *more* than these sacrifices was for His people to obey His commands, thereby avoiding sin, out of deep love for God Himself.

While social injustices and political corruption required reform (Hosea 6:8-9), they were second to God's primary concern: for the hearts of His people to be transformed, for them to love Him and have compassion for others because of their love and experience with God.[2] With this kind of heart transformation, the people's other problems would resolve.

Read Matthew 9:9-13 and Matthew 12:1-8. In both passages, who was questioning Jesus? (Note: Pharisees were experts in the Old Testament law ... and hundreds of man-made commandments they added to the law because they thought it would make them extra holy.)

The religious leaders and influencers of Jesus' time had to be reminded of the words of Hosea 6:6. The Pharisees, like Israel in Hosea's day, had grown so fond of their own ways, practices and traditions that they forgot the heart of God and His ways. Jesus used Hosea 6:6 to expose their hypocrisy.

Jesus also summed up this message later in the book of Matthew. In the midst of seven woe oracles directed to the Pharisees, Jesus warned them, *"You clean the outside of the cup and the plate, but inside they are full of greed and self-indulgence"* (Matthew 23:25). Jesus then prescribed the antidote to their hypocrisy: Clean the inside first (v. 26).

From Hosea to Jesus, the message remains the same: God wants our hearts. He's not just interested in whether or not we *look* religious. God isn't calling us to a life of empty rituals. While religious practices are good, they're meant to overflow from a heart deeply connected to Christ.

> *Describe something or someone you love and feel deeply connected to. How do you speak about that thing/person? How much time do you spend thinking about it? How do you respond when something else gets in the way of this important connection?*

> *How does the relationship you described above compare to your relationship with God?*

"Steadfast love and not sacrifice" (Hosea 6:6) means we devote all our powers and faculties to loving God, and we prefer nothing over Him.[3] Perhaps the simplest way to begin shifting our hearts toward this kind of love for God is to ask for His help. God will faithfully answer when we ask Him to give us hearts that love Him more and to peel our hearts away from the love of the world and the things in it.

Day 15 — HOSEA 7:1-10

Israel's sins were exposed, including theft, deceit and arrogance.

Have you ever had "analysis paralysis"? When we have too many options in front of us, our brains can get overwhelmed, and then it's hard to make a decision at all. But today's reading presents a simple choice: There are only two possible positions of the heart, and each position leads to a very different path.

The first heart position is unrepentance. Our reading in Hosea 7 will further illuminate the characteristics of such a heart, as well as the consequences. The second heart position is repentance ... but more on that at the end of today's study.

First, what are the three "evil deeds" of Israel listed in Hosea 7:1? How does this echo Hosea 6:7-10?

To what did Hosea compare Israel in Hosea 7:4 and Hosea 7:6-7? What do you think it means to have "hearts like an oven" (v. 6)?

While some of the verses in today's reading had the leaders of Israel specifically in view, it seems *"all of them,"* everyone, had sinful hearts that burned out of control (vv. 3-7). As Hosea also referenced the entire nation, we can conclude that in spite of the chaos and destruction caused by their sin, no one sought the Lord or called upon His name.

And sandwiched between these symptoms of Israel's unrepentant heart, Hosea stated the consequence plainly in verse 2: God would *"remember all their evil. Now their deeds surround them; they are before [God's] face."* The Hebrew phrase translated as *"their deeds surround them"* in this verse has also been translated as *"their deeds surround and entangle them"* (AMP); it is the image of a heart trapped by its own sin before a holy God. God's people were in plain view of His holy eyes, yet they continued in their wicked ways.

Describe a time when you've been caught doing something you knew was wrong. What was your response?

You may have heard that God doesn't remember sin, and you would be right that this is true for those who love Him! However, this is not the case for the unrepentant heart.

Read Micah 7:19. What does this verse say about where God will "cast all our sins"?

Now read Micah 7:18. Whose sins did Micah specifically say God would pardon and pass over?

The wages of sin is death for those who are not part of God's inheritance, meaning those who don't trust in Him for salvation. But remember there is a second heart position: repentance! The path for this heart points in a very different direction. For the repentant heart, the gift of God is eternal life through faith in Jesus (Romans 3:23-24). For the repentant heart, God forgives our sin.

Read Hebrews 8:10-12. Write down some keywords you find in these verses that remind you of truths we've studied in the book of Hosea:

The people of Hosea's time had the hope of God's salvation available to them — yet they lived entangled and mixed up with the wicked world (Hosea 7:8-10). Consequently, they would face a God who remembered their sin.

Through the author of Hebrews, God spoke of the new covenant established through Jesus. Every heart that turns to Christ receives God's promise of the most unfathomable reward: **He will remember our sins no more.** Before we expect God's reward, let's make sure we offer Him our repentance and faith. And as we do, let's celebrate the grace God extends because of His unconditional love for us.

DOESN'T GOD HAVE A PERFECT MEMORY?

Since God has all power and knowledge (Romans 11:33-36; Isaiah 46:9-11), we could say God doesn't truly forget anything. Asking whether God could choose to forget is a bit like asking whether He could create a rock He couldn't lift. God doesn't do what is outside His character: either creating or lifting impossibly heavy rocks. In the same way, even if God could intentionally forget something, He could just as intentionally remember it again. When God says, "I will remember their sins no more" (Hebrews 8:12), He is speaking to us using human concepts (remembering and forgetting) to help us understand something that is remarkably profound: By God's grace, for every believer, our sin is completely covered by the blood of Christ and therefore is completely forgiven — as good as forgotten — and never to be brought up again.

Week Three

REFLECTION *and* PRAYER

As we concluded our study this week, we read of the repeated refusal of God's people to call out to Him: *"All their kings have fallen, and none of them calls upon me"* (Hosea 7:7). Matthew Henry notes that people who are "not only heated with sin, but hardened in sin" will "continue to live without prayer, even when in trouble and distress."[1] Refusing to turn to heaven, Israel grasped for anything on earth to help her — including gods she did not know and nations that only oppressed her. Absent of prayer to the one true God, the nation was certainly doomed.

When we refuse to call out to God in prayer, we, too, are left to rely on our own devices. We have only ourselves to try to fix whatever confronts us.

Meanwhile, Jesus already came to fix it all.

Jesus' own life on earth demonstrated that prayer is a gift and a privilege. It is not a burden, nor is it simply an optional practice we pick up and put down at our convenience. Instead, it is meant to be a thread woven into the fabric of our lives.

Jesus prayed in the midst of thousands to give thanks to His Father (Matthew 14:19).
Jesus prayed in solitude to draw near to His Father (Matthew 14:23; Mark 1:35; Luke 5:16).
Jesus prayed in the final hours of His life, even when He desired for God to take away the cup of suffering that awaited Him (Matthew 26:39).

If Jesus prayed continually and about everything, let's do the same as we love and follow Him (Ephesians 6:18). As Hosea said, *"Let us know; let us press on to know the LORD"* (Hosea 6:3).

We can start right now.

Dear God, forgive me for the many times I have turned to something else instead of calling to You in my time of need. Whether searching the internet or mustering up my own best efforts ... I confess now that nothing but You could ever fix the brokenness of my circumstances or the sickness of my heart. Alert me when I look to anything but You for guidance, provision, protection or comfort. I want to taste and see that You are good, and I want to experience Your presence. In Jesus' name, amen.

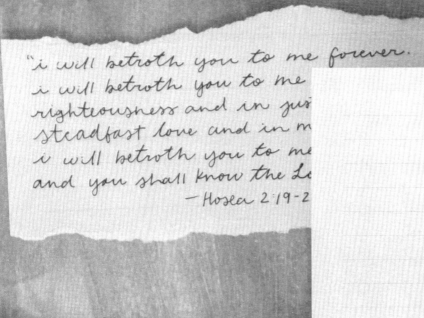

"i will betroth you to me forever.
i will betroth you to me [in]
righteousness and in jus[tice, in]
steadfast love and in m[ercy.]
i will betroth you to me [in faithfulness]
and you shall know the Lo[rd.]"
— Hosea 2:19-2[0]

Kirkpatrick

275   From The D[epths]

Psalm 130. 8s and 7s.

1. From the depths do   I   in-voke Thee,
2. Lord, if Thou shouldst mark transgressions
3. For   Je - ho - vah   I   am wait-ing, [A]
4. For   the Lord my   soul is wait-ing M[y]

To   my voice be   Thou at - ten - tive A[s]
But with Thee there is   for-give-ness, T[hat]
In   His word of   promise giv - en, Y[es]
More than they for   morning watching, W[ith]

CHORUS

Is - r'el hope thou   in   Je - ho - vah,   Mercies   great are found with Him;

righteou[s]
steadfas[t]
l will b[etroth]
faithfu[l]

NOTES

NOTES

NOTES

NOTES

Day 16 — HOSEA 7:11-16

Israelites cried out on their beds but said "no" to God in their hearts.

Jumping into the ocean in the state of Maine *any* time of year is bound to give you a slight shock. The highest average ocean temperature there is 68 degrees Fahrenheit at the height of summer. Since water conducts heat away from the body faster than air, 68-degree water is cold! Jumping into Hosea 7 this week may also feel like jumping into some icy water. Hosea 7 concludes with a woe oracle where God continued to lament the rebellious nature of His people.

In Hosea 7:13, the ESV Bible says, *"Woe to them, for they have strayed from me!"* Some translators suggest the original language was even more forceful and are inclined to render it as *"they fled from me"* (CSB) to capture the thought that Israel was not just unknowingly straying but actively choosing to run away from God.[1]

Israel turned to other nations for help instead of turning from her sin (Hosea 7:11). She corrupted herself with other gods and indulged in her evil desires, and as a result, she would become *"like a treacherous bow"* (v. 16). The word *"treacherous"* in this verse can also be translated as *"faulty"* (NIV) or *"defective"* (NRSVA). It gives us the image of a useless bow that will miss the mark every time.

Though God Himself had *"trained and strengthened"* Israel (v. 15), the people forgot His past faithfulness and now turned to wage war against the very One who had made them into warriors. They lost sight of their God-given identity and purpose.

Let's read Joshua 21:43-45, which describes events about 700 years before Hosea's lifetime, and then answer the questions below.

- *According to Joshua 21:43, who had given Israel the land in which they were currently living in Hosea's day?*

- *After the Israelites took possession of the land and settled in it, what did God give them in Joshua 21:44?*

- *How many of their enemies had withstood them (Joshua 21:44)? Why?*

- *Write Joshua 21:45 in the space below:*

After all God had done for Israel, Judges 2:10 points to the sad truth that set the stage for where we find Israel in the book of Hosea: *"All that generation also were gathered to their fathers. And there arose another generation after them who did not know the LORD or the work that he had done for Israel."*

Generations of God's people failed to pass on the knowledge of His love and faithfulness. Consequently, they relied on other nations and false gods. Even when they were desperate, they *"wail[ed] upon their beds"* but did not cry out to God *"from the heart"* (Hosea 7:14).

*What is the distinction between simply **crying** versus **crying out to God?** Why is it important to know the difference?*

Maybe we hope to pass on life skills like how to change the oil in a car or use a sewing machine. Sometimes we pass on habits or recipes for our favorite dishes. But none of those things will matter if we neglect to pass on the Truth about the only God who can save and rescue in times of trouble. Let us be a generation that speaks of His love and faithfulness — not with arbitrary words but from the heart, sharing our personal experiences of His love.

As God trained and strengthened Israel (Hosea 7:15), God trains and strengthens us today *"to make [us] wise for salvation through faith in Christ Jesus … equipped for every good work"* (2 Timothy 3:15-17). We are called to acknowledge His work in our lives and share it with those who come behind us so they may:

· Know the Truth, not lies (Hosea 7:13).

· Cry out to God from the heart instead of wailing without hope (Hosea 7:14).

· Return to God in true faith when sin leads them astray (Hosea 7:16).

Below, write a prayer asking God to give you the opportunity to speak of His love and faithfulness today.

Day 17 — Hosea 8:1-6

Israel once claimed to know God yet worshipped a golden calf.

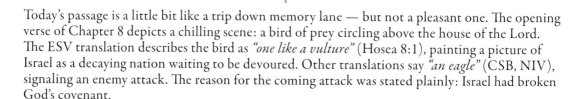

Today's passage is a little bit like a trip down memory lane — but not a pleasant one. The opening verse of Chapter 8 depicts a chilling scene: a bird of prey circling above the house of the Lord. The ESV translation describes the bird as *"one like a vulture"* (Hosea 8:1), painting a picture of Israel as a decaying nation waiting to be devoured. Other translations say *"an eagle"* (CSB, NIV), signaling an enemy attack. The reason for the coming attack was stated plainly: Israel had broken God's covenant.

Though the words of God's covenant had grown dim in the thoughts of His people, scholars agree that His law, as recorded in books like Deuteronomy, likely rang in Hosea's ears as he wrote this passage. Deuteronomy 28:26 and Deuteronomy 28:49 offer similar images of birds devouring the disobedient.

In response to the alarm and impending destruction in Hosea 8:1, Hosea recorded a cry for help — *"my God"* — as Israel appeared to acknowledge the Lord in verse 2. But her cry was not sincere. It's possible Israel actually *believed* she knew God, but her worship of Him had become so mingled with her worship of Baal that she could not *truly know* God. This is the danger of syncretism, as we defined on Page 13 of this study. Scholar Thomas McComiskey goes so far as to say, "They did not know the ways of Yahweh. They knew better the ways of Baal."[1]

According to Hosea 8:3, what had Israel spurned?

The good Israel rejected was more than just the opposite of evil. It represented God's covenant and everything He wanted to do for His people if they obeyed it.[2]

Read Deuteronomy 30:9-10 and verses 15-16. What are some of the good things God promised His people if they were faithful to the covenant?

What choice did God set before His people in Deuteronomy 30:15?

What did God require from Israel in Deuteronomy 30:16 to receive His good blessings of life?

Sadly, the people failed to hold up their end of the covenant. Over time, their worship of God became so intertwined with worship of false gods that they could no longer distinguish between what was real and what was not. God's repeated attempts to wake up His people fell on dull minds and hard hearts until finally He resolved to break the nation, along with her idols, *"to pieces"* (Hosea 8:6).

What does Hosea 8:5 specifically say God spurned?

The calf mentioned in Hosea 8:5-6 could point toward two instances of idolatry in Israel's history:

1. While Moses received the Ten Commandments from God on Mount Sinai, God's people grew impatient and formed a calf idol to worship in the wilderness (Exodus 32).

2. In their more recent history, when the nation split, King Jeroboam of Israel made two calf idols and placed them in Bethel and Dan. He compelled the people of Israel not to go down to Jerusalem (in the southern kingdom of Judah) to offer sacrifices to the true God at His temple (1 Kings 12:28-29).

Whether God was referencing one or both of these golden calves, His four-word assertion about the calf of Samaria in Hosea 8:6 cannot be confused: *"It is not God."*

What kinds of "calves" do you see in the world today that people worship and treat as gods but are not truly God? What about in your own community or your own life?

Let's embrace this passage as an invitation to discover and nurture an authentic relationship with God — one that will never *"be broken to pieces"* (v. 6). By looking for things we might inadvertently elevate above (or even put on the same level with!) our relationship with God, we can determine to intentionally realign our priorities and ensure our worship and devotion are centered on Him.

Day 18 — HOSEA 8:7-14

Israel's reliance on foreign alliances was like sowing seed in the wind.

———— ✳ ————

Hosea described Israel in both new and familiar ways in today's reading. In this passage, we see Israel compared to *"a useless vessel"* (Hosea 8:8) and *"a wild donkey wandering alone"* (v. 9) in her pursuit of foreign nations for defense. She also took pride and sought refuge in her own provisions (v. 14). Yet Hosea foretold that her hollow hopes would betray her, and she would reap no good harvest because she had sown no good seed (v. 7).

Hosea 8:11 says, "Because Ephraim has multiplied altars for sinning, they have become to him altars for sinning." If this seems a bit redundant, try reading the verse in another translation like the NLT. How does this further show the irony and futility of sin?

All the while, God had given Israel plentiful principles, commands and directions regarding every aspect of life to provide for her freedom and abundance. If only she had lived by these laws of love! Yet she gave God's Word no regard — or worse, she regarded it as foreign. God lamented, *"Were I to write for [Israel] my laws by the ten thousands, they would be regarded as a strange thing"* (v. 12).

In contrast to Israel's relationship with God's Word in Hosea 8, let's look at some other possible approaches to Scripture. In Psalm 119:11, what did the psalmist say he did with God's Word? Why?

The ancient image presented in Psalm 119:11 is that of a storage chest where someone would have kept possessions of great value, like treasure. Jesus also drew on this image when He talked about the Kingdom of God.

Read Matthew 13:44. What did Jesus say the Kingdom of heaven is like? What did the man who found the treasure do in response to his discovery?

Both of these examples, in the Old Testament and the New Testament, depict people who understand the value of God's Word and rightly respond by treasuring it. The psalmist stored up the Word in his heart so he could live in obedience to God's commands. The man in Jesus' parable joyfully gave up anything that stood in the way of his partaking of the treasures of heaven.

How do you approach God's Word? Do you consider it an afterthought, something you are only occasionally concerned with? Or is it something you store up as a treasure?

In Hosea's day, God's people who stubbornly ignored His Word were *"sow[ing] the wind,"* and Hosea 8:7 prophesied that they would *"reap the whirlwind"* of conquest and exile to Assyria, which eventually happened in 2 Kings 17:1-18.

Centuries later, the Apostle Paul also taught about reaping what we sow, saying, *"The one who sows to his own flesh will from the flesh reap corruption, but the one who sows to the Spirit will from the Spirit reap eternal life"* (Galatians 6:8).

Certainly we want to avoid the consequences so clearly connected to sowing to the flesh. Yet somehow this pattern of sin has repeated itself over centuries. Thankfully, there is a way to break the pattern and avoid reaping corruption: We can choose to sow to the Holy Spirit! To reap eternal life, we treasure the Word of God and trust in Jesus, the Word Himself who came and dwelled among us in God's greatest act of love (John 1:14). And as we treasure God's Word and learn His ways, we also share His love with others.

Day 19 — Hosea 9:1-9

Israel saw prophets, channels of God's Word, as foolish.

Yesterday we read Hosea 8:7, which said of Israel, *"They sow the wind, and they shall reap the whirlwind."* As we begin Hosea 9, this harvest — or lack of it — is in view. In today's passage, Hosea prophesied about a famine that would come upon the land and ultimately give way to war and exile.

The people of Israel ordinarily would have celebrated the abundance of a harvest, but as we've seen already in Hosea, they were not accrediting their provisions to God and instead were praising pagan gods. Therefore, God said in Hosea 9:2 that He would withdraw His hand of provision, and their crops would fail. Instead of rejoicing, they would return to bondage and hunger as in the days of their slavery in Egypt, and their bread would be *"like mourners' bread"* (Hosea 9:3-4).

Mourners' bread implied a time of famine — a time where death would be so prevalent that contact with the dead, which caused ceremonial uncleanness or contamination according to God's law (Leviticus 21:11; Numbers 5:2), would be common, and even food would be affected. Unclean bread was not suitable for use in the house of the Lord.[1]

Interestingly, scholars also suggest that Hosea 9:1 may be a reversal of a typical ancient harvest proclamation. The usual proclamation may have been something like, "Rejoice, Israel, for Yahweh has given you a harvest!" But by saying, *"Rejoice not, O Israel!"* (v. 1), Hosea took a proclamation of joy and turned it into a lament.[2]

Hosea also described Israel as *"play[ing] the whore, forsaking [her] God"* (v. 1); she expected pagan fertility gods to make her fields prosper, yet they had left her barren. No longer would the people rejoice at the harvest. No longer would they celebrate at their festivals (v. 5).

According to verse 7, how did the people regard prophets like Hosea in these "days of punishment"?

Verse 8 tells us the truth about God's prophets: What does this verse say "the prophet is"?

Judgment was now upon Israel, but it didn't have to be this way. Had the people received Hosea as the watchman God appointed him to be, they would have heeded his words and considered them wisdom, not foolishness.

Read Matthew 5:11-12, an excerpt from Jesus' well-known Sermon on the Mount. What circumstances did Jesus tell His disciples they should consider a blessing? Why?

Who did Jesus prompt His disciples to remember as examples of this kind of blessing?

Just as Hosea and other Old Testament prophets endured trials because of their *obedience* to God, disciples of Jesus can expect the same kinds of trouble. But these troubles reap far different results than suffering for *disobedience*, as the Israelites of Hosea's time did.

The Israelites rejected God and would not rejoice in their harvest in Hosea 9:1-4. But as disciples of Jesus, what can we count as joy, according to James 1:2-4?

The Israelites put their faith in the gods of their culture and ultimately lost hope of provision and purity (Hosea 9:6). But for disciples of Jesus, what does suffering produce, according to Romans 5:3-4?

Because of their sin, Israel would eat mourners' bread (Hosea 9:4). But Jesus, who forgives the sins of all who trust in Him, says: *"Blessed are those who mourn, for they shall be comforted"* (Matthew 5:4).

Today, may we choose not to rejoice over empty, earthly things that will only fade away. Instead, may we humble ourselves before a holy, loving God and grieve our sin so we can rejoice in His comfort and find hope in His perfect love.

Israel's history of unfaithfulness led to God's expressions of anger.

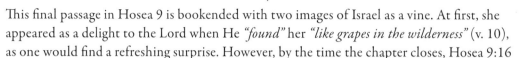

This final passage in Hosea 9 is bookended with two images of Israel as a vine. At first, she appeared as a delight to the Lord when He *"found"* her *"like grapes in the wilderness"* (v. 10), as one would find a refreshing surprise. However, by the time the chapter closes, Hosea 9:16 describes how Israel later became like a dried-up root that would not bear fruit.

Hosea 9:10 points to the cause of the vine's withering, which began long ago, even before Israel entered the promised land: *"But they came to Baal-peor and consecrated themselves to the thing of shame ..."* This refers to the events of Numbers 25:1-9, when Israelites had sexual relations with Moabite women who worshipped Baal-peor, and as judgment for their sins, God sent a plague that killed 24,000 Israelites. This may seem like a shocking consequence — and it is. In fact, it prompts us to ask: How many lives might have been *saved* in Israel if the people were *more* shocked by the destructiveness of sin? This was part of God's loving intention as He delivered justice.

Psalm 106 also tells of this stain on Israel's history.

Read Psalm 106:28-30 and Psalm 106:36-39. What did the worship of Baal-peor include?

How does this relate to Hosea 9:13? Who was responsible for leading their own children to death?

Psalm 106:39 describes Israel's actions in two ways: *"They became unclean by their acts, and played the whore in their deeds."* Scholar Duane Garrett states, "The psalm thus brings out the hideous paradox of the fertility cult: a major objective of the cult was to enable women to give birth to many healthy children, but that same cult consumed children in ritual sacrifice."[1]

While it is heartbreaking to consider the horrors of Israel's alignment with Baal, it is important for our understanding of God's long-suffering patience, justice and love.

How did the people's actions concerning Baal-peor affect them, according to Hosea 9:10c?

The phrase *"became detestable like the thing they loved"* asserts that the people took on the character of the cult. They became like their idols. Therefore, they became detestable to God, and He would *"depart from them"* (v. 12).[2] This brings us to the final image of Israel as a barren vineyard — a metaphor that pictured the end of the nation as they knew it (v. 16). Although we know God promised future restoration for His people elsewhere in the book of Hosea, as we close Chapter 9, we find no such promise. Today's passage includes some extremely difficult prophecies, and it does not resolve with a happy ending.

But even this can ultimately help us grasp the depth of God's glorious, unconditional love — in contrast to the depth of the hopelessness of sin. The more God reveals the consequences of sin, we more deeply long for and appreciate His loving forgiveness.

We can also see this clearly in the words of Isaiah 64:6:

*"For we have **all** become like one who is unclean [ceremonially, like a leper], and **all** our righteousness (our best deeds of rightness and justice) is like filthy rags or a polluted garment; we **all** fade like a leaf, and our iniquities, like the wind, take us away [far from God's favor, hurrying us toward destruction]"* (AMPC, emphases added).

Three times in this verse, Isaiah recorded truths about us "all." Paraphrase those three truths below:

1.

2.

3.

What does Isaiah 64:6 say our iniquities do?

Finally, now read Isaiah 64:8. What does this verse declare to be true despite our sin and brokenness? How does this truth shape your reading of Hosea?

The Surprising Ways God Loves Us

As we read Hosea, some of what we read may not feel very loving. The way God's love is communicated in Hosea often doesn't sound the same as the famous words of 1 Corinthians 13:4-7: *"Love is patient and kind; love does not envy or boast; it is not arrogant or rude. It does not insist on its own way; it is not irritable or resentful; it does not rejoice at wrongdoing, but rejoices with the truth. Love bears all things, believes all things, hopes all things, endures all things."* But the love of God — and even the discipline connected to His love — is faithfully consistent throughout Scripture.

The author of Hebrews, for instance, encouraged early Christians to lean into God's correction or discipline as a sign of His love. The Greek word for "discipline," which is repeated eight times in just six verses in Hebrews 12:5-10, carries the idea of training that molds the character of a person.

Hebrews 12 gives us several key indicators of how God's discipline is connected to His love:

FIRST, GOD'S DISCIPLINE POINTS TO OUR ADOPTION AS HIS CHILDREN. *"God is treating you as sons. For what son is there whom his father does not discipline?"* (Hebrews 12:7). Paul elaborated on this idea of sonship in his letter to Christians in Rome, saying followers of Christ *"have received the Spirit of adoption as sons, by whom we cry, 'Abba! Father!'"* (Romans 8:15). Jesus, God's Son, called His Father by this exact same name in one of His most desperate moments on earth — in the garden of Gethsemane, where He pleaded, *"Abba, Father, all things are possible for you. Remove this cup from me. Yet not what I will, but what you will"* (Mark 14:36).

SECOND, THERE IS A DIFFERENCE BETWEEN GOD'S PUNISHMENT FOR SIN AND GOD'S DISCIPLINE. The cup of God's wrath that Jesus drank was not punishment for His own sins. He had no sin; He suffered the punishment for *our sins* on the cross, and through faith in Him, we now have eternal access to and relationship with God. When believers experience difficulty, we can therefore understand that we are not being punished: Jesus already took our punishment, and He is the perfecter of our faith, not us (Hebrews 12:2). We cannot add any payment to the fine Jesus paid for us. For this reason, we can make a distinction between punishment and discipline. God is not angry with believers. For those in Christ, God's wrath has been satisfied on the cross.

THIRD, GOD'S DISCIPLINE HAS PURPOSE. Since God works all things together for the good of those who love Him and are called according to His purpose (Romans 8:28), we know any hardship we endure is allowed and used by God. This includes God's discipline, which is like that of a loving parent or coach training us in the right ways to live. We endure God's discipline knowing it is proof of His love and attention: *"He disciplines us for our good, that we may share his holiness"* (Hebrews 12:10). God's purpose is to make us holy as He is holy, rescuing us from the corruption of the world (1 Corinthians 11:32; 2 Peter 1:4). Titus 2:12 expands on this idea, saying that by God's grace, He is *"training us to renounce ungodliness and worldly passions, and to live self-controlled, upright, and godly lives."*

Because God takes sin seriously and knows it is harmful to us, His love takes the form of correction when we do wrong. We are not to make light of our sin, but we also do not lose heart. Instead, we can willingly submit to God and learn from His discipline. Though it may not feel loving at the time, we can be sure His discipline is for our good and look forward to *"the peaceful fruit of righteousness"* it will provide (Hebrews 12:11).

Week Four

REFLECTION *and* PRAYER

Listening can take on a variety of definitions. Sometimes we say "I'm listening" even while we watch television or scroll on our phones. Other times we say "I'm listening" as we move back and forth between rooms.

Maybe you've tried to get someone to listen to you before by following them around, keeping your voice close to their ears even as they seemed to pay you little regard. Maybe you've asked, "Are you actually hearing me?" because although they *said* they were listening, their attention appeared to be divided.

Hosea 9 closed by reiterating, *"My God will reject [Israel] because **they have not listened** to him"* (v. 17, emphasis added).

To listen to God is not the same as merely hearing Him. We may hear His voice in passing, but to listen, understand and obey requires more from us. To truly listen, we need to engage our ears, our eyes, and our hearts and minds. As we listen with our ears, we close our mouths so we don't interrupt Him. We listen with our eyes by giving our attention and focus to the One who is speaking, and we listen with our hearts and minds by thinking about what He says.

Friend, as we close this week's study, let's listen to God: being still in His presence, fixing our eyes on His Word, and thinking on His Truth.

Let's begin our time of prayer by simply being silent before the Lord. Try to do this for at least 30-60 seconds before praying the words below.

Dear God, there is nothing that could ever fill our deepest longings like Your love does. How unfathomable it is that a sinner like me could come into Your presence. Thank You for never giving up on me. I ask You to bring up Your Word continually in my heart so I may think on it and act according to Your will. In Jesus' name, amen.

"i will betroth you to me forever.
i will betroth you to me
righteousness and in ju
steadfast love and in m
i will betroth you to me
and you shall know the Lo
— Hosea 2:19-2

rkpatrick

e ear;
word,

near.
Lord.

I stand?
night,

mmand.
light..

275   From The D

Psalm 130. 8s and 7s.

1. From the depths do   I in-voke Thee,
2. Lord, if Thou shouldst mark transgressions
3. For   Je - ho - vah   I   am wait-ing,
4. For   the Lord my   soul is wait-ing M

To   my voice be   Thou at-ten-tive A
But with Thee there is   for-give-ness, Th
In   His word of   promise giv-en,   Y
More than they for   morning watching, W

CHORUS

Is - r'el hope thou   in   Je - ho - vah,   Mercies   great are found with Him;

righteou
steadfas
l will be
faithfu

NOTES

NOTES

NOTES

NOTES

WEEK FIVE

Day 21 — Hosea 10:1-8

Israel's luxuries led to increased idolatry.

If you've ever looked up in the middle of a mess and wondered, *How did I get here?*, you can likely identify with Israel at this point. After nine chapters that have revealed the apostasy of Israel's heart, it's still hard to imagine how God's people got here. It seems they needed a reminder themselves, as they were saying: *"We have no king, for we do not fear the Lord; and a king—**what could he do for us?**"* (Hosea 10:3, emphasis added).

Here's a review of just a few victories God had already secured for His people as their King:

- God delivered His people from captivity in the land of Egypt, and they witnessed Him defeat the Egyptian army after they walked through the Red Sea on dry land (Exodus 14:26-29).
- The people watched God overcome more enemies, like how He strengthened Israel's armies to defeat the Amalekites as Moses lifted up his hands on a hill (Exodus 17:8-14).
- At Jericho, God told His people to march around an enemy city, then shout and watch as the city's walls crumbled before them (Joshua 6).
- God later brought deliverance through leaders known as "judges"; for example, Gideon was the weakest and the least, yet with God's help, he defeated the Midianite army with only 300 men (Judges 6-7).

Despite this history of prosperity and protection under God's leadership, Hosea 10:1-2 traces the story of how Israel fell so far away from God. As she experienced God's blessings, she used her wealth (*"fruit"*) to make altars and pillars for idol worship. Her heart was false, and she *"improved"* with her own interests in view, not pleasing God and serving Him. Consequently, the people would have to *"bear their guilt."*

Verses 5-6 say that God's chosen people living in Samaria, brought by His hand into the land He gave them, now trembled and mourned before a lifeless statue of a calf. They experienced the shame of defeat because an idol made by humans could do nothing to save them.

One scholar notes that Israel ironically was not seized by a sense of shame when the people partnered with cult prostitutes, violated the purity of their God-given traditions, or lied and cheated for profit — it required the final consequences of their waywardness for them to finally see the end result of their folly. Only then were they ashamed.[1]

We see a similar shame over sin in Romans 7:24, when the Apostle Paul was so guilt-ridden that he cried out, "Wretched man that I am! Who will deliver me from this body of death?" *But what did Paul cry out in Romans 7:25a?*

What does this teach us about how God reveals our guilt so He can redeem us from it?

According to Hosea 10:8, what would Israel say when faced with the guilt and consequences of her actions?

These words of Hosea 10:8 also appear twice in the New Testament.

As Jesus was led to the cross to die as the sacrificial Lamb of God and take away the sins of the world, He quoted Hosea 10:8 as He issued a warning to the large number of people who followed Him: Destruction and despair await those who refuse His love.

Read Luke 23:26-31. What similarities do you see in how the people of Hosea's time rejected God and how the people of Jesus' time rejected Him?

Next, Hosea 10:8 is also referenced in Revelation 6:12-17, a prophecy of how Jesus will bring justice for all sin at the end of time.

Who will call to the mountains and rocks to hide them, according to Revelation 6:15? Who will they try to hide from, and why, in Revelation 6:16-17?

For a phrase like this to be repeated three times in Scripture, we would be prudent to take it to heart. We, like Israel, have a choice to receive God's love or reject it. Hosea 10:2 cautions us not to make this choice with a divided and deceitful heart, and Hosea 10:4 echoes that lip service and *"empty oaths"* are not accepted by a holy God.

But because of God's great love for us, there is a way we will never have to *"say to the mountains, 'Cover us'"*(Hosea 10:8)! When we turn to Jesus in faith, our lives become hidden in Christ (Colossians 3:3), and His love *"covers a multitude of sins"* (1 Peter 4:8).

Day 22 — Hosea 10:9-15

Among warnings of utter destruction, God pleaded for Israel to seek after Him.

———————— ✳ ————————

Today's reading returns to agricultural metaphors to help us understand God's relationship with His people (who were mostly farmers — so even the type of metaphor God chose here reveals His desire to connect with them!). Hosea portrayed Israel as a luxuriant vine in the opening verse of yesterday's reading (Hosea 10:1). Now he identified her as a calf, capable and willing to plow fields for harvest — but she only planted bad seed (Hosea 10:11; Hosea 10:13).

What kind of fruit did this seed produce in verse 13?

Because of how they *"plowed iniquity"* (v. 13), Hosea did not hold out hope that the imminent judgment of God's people would change. But he did hope for a future return to the Lord. With that hope in view, Hosea gave Israel a road map for the way back.

Fill in the blanks of Hosea 10:12 below with the directives Hosea gave Israel:

"_____ for yourselves righteousness; _____ steadfast love; _____

_____ your fallow ground, for it is the time to _____ the Lord ..."

Here we see three clear steps of repentance and redemption:

FIRST, SOW RIGHTEOUSNESS TO REAP STEADFAST LOVE. God Himself is the source and the essence of righteousness, or the "standard of fairness and equity that is essential to the divine character."[1] Israel's necessary response to maintain their relationship with their covenant God was to live in accordance to His standards and reap His loyal love.[2]

SECOND, BEGIN ANEW. Fallow farmland was left uncultivated and unsown, so the phrase *"break up your fallow ground"* (v. 12) points to the preparation of new soil for planting. For Israel, this meant they were to renounce their old ways and open new "fields" of obedience to God. In the New Testament, Paul wrote about this as *"put[ting] off your old self, which belongs to your former manner of life and is corrupt through deceitful desires ... to put on the new self, created after the likeness of God in true righteousness and holiness"* (Ephesians 4.22-24).

FINALLY, SEEK THE LORD. To seek the Lord is to turn to Him in faith, prayer and obedience. Bible commentator Matthew Henry points out that this "is to be every day's work ... If we sow in righteousness, we shall reap according to mercy; a reward not of debt, but of grace."[3]

Describe what "every day's work" looks like for you currently. What would it look like for seeking the Lord to be your spiritual work every day?

As we consider the ideas of sowing and reaping, let's also read Galatians 5:22-24. What are some specific examples of how God has produced this spiritual fruit in your life as you seek Him?

What fruit have you seen in your life that is not fruit of the Spirit? What "seeds" have you sown in the soil of your heart that may be the root of this undesired fruit?

The fruit we produce is easily identifiable evidence of whether we are truly seeking and trusting God. A lack of good fruit can also show us where problem areas lie. Our prescription for solving these problems, however, is often wrong. We tend to focus on a change in behavior, but what we need first is a change of heart. We cannot expect to reap righteousness, love and peace yet continue to trust in our own ways. And a harvest of injustice won't change if we busy ourselves with trying to make it right while still sowing seeds of iniquity.

Thank God that He gives us grace we don't deserve: His rain of righteousness (Hosea 10:12). In ancient Israel, this rain would quench the thirst of parched souls and satisfy His people's longings. God Himself would provide what was necessary for His people to experience abundant harvest — and He will do the same for us today.

Day 23 — Hosea 11:1-7

Despite God's love and care, Israel would make Assyria their king.

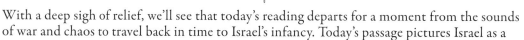

With a deep sigh of relief, we'll see that today's reading departs for a moment from the sounds of war and chaos to travel back in time to Israel's infancy. Today's passage pictures Israel as a son, with God as his Father. The language in this chapter demonstrates great tenderness, and it stands out as one of the most vivid descriptions of God's love in the Old Testament.[1]

Record some of the words that reflect God's gentle care and love for His people in Hosea 11:1-4.

These verses recall God's words to Moses in Exodus 4:22: *"Thus says the Lord, Israel is my firstborn son."* It also marks a shift away from the metaphor of Israel as a wife unfaithful to God, her husband, which has predominated the book of Hosea. Now God said, *"When Israel was a child, I loved him "* (Hosea 11:1).

Sadly, God also said of His children, *"They did not know that I healed them"* (v. 3), a phrase that looks back again to Israel's exodus from Egypt. The exodus was fundamental in Israel's understanding and knowledge of God, and here, Hosea reflected on the nation's history to remind the people of the God they once knew.

Read Exodus 15:22-26. How did God reveal Himself to Israel in verse 26?

Jehovah-Rapha in Hebrew, which means "The Lord Who Heals," describes God as the One who mends and tends to all the needs of His people — physical, emotional and spiritual. Hosea had already pointed out that the Israelites in his day did not recognize God's care for them (Hosea 2:5; Hosea 2:8). Now we see how far back in Israel's history this misplaced confidence went.

Hosea 11:4 continues the remembrance of the exodus experience; however, the metaphor changes from Israel as a son to Israel as an ox that God gently led.

What two things did God lead Israel "with" in verse 4?

What did God say He "became to them" *(v. 4)?*

A yoke normally refers to a wooden beam placed across the neck of a working farm animal to make it yield to the farmer's direction. The *"yoke on their jaws"* in verse 4 likely refers to a horse's bit, which serves a similar purpose. To *"eas[e] the yoke"* (v. 4) here refers to how God lifted the oppressive burden of slavery Israel endured while in Egypt (Leviticus 26:13).

It's interesting to note the text does not say God removed all yokes, or all direction, entirely — but instead He eased the yoke. What did Jesus say about an easy yoke in Matthew 11:28-30? How does this echo and fulfill Hosea 11?

Israel could have accepted the ease of God's yoke — yet because the people *"refused to return"* to God, they would return to slavery like in Egypt, but this time in Assyria (Hosea 11:5). War would swirl around them. The city gates they put their hopes in for protection would crash to the ground (v. 6). God's people were determined to desert Him. The Father who so dearly loved them. The One who called them. The One who taught them to walk. The One who healed them. The One who led them and fed them (vv. 1-4).

Like Israel, we will all be yoked to something or by someone. We can struggle daily beneath the yoke of our sin and shame, or we can come to Jesus and take His yoke as beloved children of God. Jesus' yoke is easy, and His burden is light. He will gently teach and guide us. He will give us rest for our souls.

How will you take the yoke of Jesus today?

DAY 24 — HOSEA 11:8-12

God's compassion tempered His judgment.

———— ❖ ————

Along with foresight of the consequences that awaited His beloved people, today's reading gives us a glimpse into God's heart in a way we have not yet seen in the book of Hosea: *"My heart recoils within me; my compassion grows warm and tender"* (Hosea 11:8). What an expression of honest despair and emotion that we as humans can understand.

While God is *"not a man"* (Hosea 11:9), and His character and ways are not bound by our understanding, we can take these words for what they are: a revelation of the depths of God's love for His people and an expression of pain for what He knew they would endure because of their stubborn hearts.

How does this expression of God's heart in Hosea 11:8-9 impact your perspective on Him and His love?

God's deep lament concluded with an expression of grace: *"I will not execute my burning anger ... I will not come in wrath"* (Hosea 11:9). God would not altogether give up His people.

At first, this might sound like a contradiction after all God's promises to judge Israel leading up to this verse — but let's look closer. Israel's choices warranted God giving them up entirely. Wrath is what they deserved. It is what they chose. Yet God in His unconditional love would not hand them over to *total* destruction.

The reference to Admah and Zeboiim in Hosea 11:8 is also important: Long ago, God *did totally destroy* these evil cities along with Sodom and Gomorrah in Genesis 19:23-29 (see also Deuteronomy 29:23). In Hosea's day, while God would not remove the punishment of exile for His people, He vowed not to destroy the nation of Israel completely, as He had destroyed Sodom, Gomorrah and the cities of the plain.

In Hosea 11:9, what did God say was the reason He would not execute the fullness of His judgment on Israel?

Israel knew God as *"the Holy One"* (v. 9), separate or set apart from all others. To say that God is holy expresses His pure and perfect nature, unstained by sin and evil, always right and good.[1] God's people were taught to obey His law because of His holiness and were themselves called to be holy as He is holy (Leviticus 11:44-45; Leviticus 19:2).

Read Isaiah 6:1-4. Describe in your own words what you read in these verses.

What do you notice about Isaiah's response to God's holiness in Isaiah 6:5?

The holiness of God requires righteousness. At the same time, God's holiness is the reason He would not carry out the full measure of His wrath upon unrighteous Israel. While Hosea didn't know all of God's plan for redemption ... God knew His own Son, Jesus, would one day bear the punishment for sin and completely satisfy God's wrath against it.

Read Romans 3:23-25 and 2 Corinthians 5:21. How do these verses relate to Hosea 11:9?

God temporarily restrained the fullness of His wrath from pouring out on Israel, and even better than that, He eternally averts His wrath from us as believers in Jesus. Our rebellious hearts chose God's wrath and deserved it, yet our holy God allowed His Son to bear what we could not bear so that we could enter into an intimate relationship with Him.

The final verses of Hosea 11 envision Israel's return to God. God's people *"shall come trembling"* in response to His call (vv. 10-11). Matthew Henry explains how this, too, points to Jesus: "Christ has purchased the pardon, and he has promised it. Holy trembling at the word of Christ will draw us to him, not drive us from him ... [We] flee to him."[2]

How will you come trembling to Jesus today?

DOES GOD HAVE A HEART?

As we read verses like Hosea 11:8, we might ask ourselves, If God is holy and completely different from humankind, how does He have a heart and feel emotions? *This is a good question to ask — even if we can't fully answer it in our limited understanding. It's a blessing to contemplate the nature of our great God.*

One of His divine attributes is impassibility, meaning God is not subject to emotional change like we are. This doesn't mean God is emotionless, but His emotions are not volatile passions: They are perfect, infinite and constant. Let's take love, for example: "If God is impassible, then he does not merely possess love, he is love ... He cannot become more loving than he already is eternally. If he did, then his love would be passible, it would change, perhaps from good to better, which would imply it was not perfect to begin with."[3]

The language in Hosea 11:8 is also an example of accommodation: Though the fullness of God transcends our understanding, He accommodates our human limitations by revealing Himself to us in some ways we can comprehend. God was not saying in Hosea 11:8 that He had a literal human heart beating in His chest, but He was revealing His love for His people.

Day 25 — Hosea 12:1-6

God recalled Israel's beginnings to remind the people He was their Helper.

After the gentle reminders of God's deep love for His people in Chapter 11, in today's reading, Hosea returned to focus on the rebellion of the people and the punishment required by a holy God. The Lord *"ha[d] an indictment"* against Israel and Judah (Hosea 12:2).

In Hosea 12:2, God said He would punish and repay Judah and Jacob according to what?

This reminds us God's punishment was never excessive or uncalled for: It was fitting and proportional *"according to"* His people's crimes of disobedience, including social injustice and idolatry.

Following God's charge against Jacob (meaning all of Israel) in verse 2, Hosea turned — somewhat abruptly — to summarize the life of Jacob himself as an ancestor of Israel.

Three scenes emerge in these two verses recounting Jacob's life:

1. First, Hosea 12:3 gives brief details about Jacob's birth. Jacob was a twin, and Scripture notes that he wrestled with his brother, Esau, in the womb (Genesis 25:22-26).

2. Hosea 12:4 recounts how, later in life, Jacob wrestled or *"strove"* with God and received a blessing from Him (Genesis 32:22-32).

3. At Bethel, as mentioned in Hosea 12:4, God passed His covenant promise to Jacob, who ultimately became the father of the 12 tribes of Israel (Genesis 28:10-22).

Scholars differ on exactly why they believe Hosea focused on Jacob in this oracle, but the themes of wrestling and receiving God's promises seem significant. Perhaps Hosea desired to remind the people of Jacob's persevering spirit, with the hope of imploring them to follow his example. Thomas McComiskey notes, "It is as though Hosea recalls these events in order to provide an emotional basis for his plea. He holds before the people the memory of their ancestor who prevailed with God; could they not also prevail with God?"[1] A second idea could be that Hosea wanted to show how Jacob's struggles gave way to him receiving grace — not by his own striving but as a gift of God.[2]

Whatever Hosea's reasons for recounting these scenes from Jacob's life, his predominant purpose was to tell the story of the God who met Jacob: *"the Lord, the God of hosts ... your God"* (Hosea 12:5-6). The title *"God of hosts"* emphasizes God's sovereign rule over all creation and powers in the universe, including angels; heavenly and terrestrial armies; the stars, sun and moon; and more. It was this God of Hosts who blessed Jacob and remained faithful to him.

With this in view, Hosea again called to the people of Israel to return to Him. What three directives did Hosea give the people in Hosea 12:6?

The familiar word *"return"* in verse 6 called for the people to abandon their false gods, repent and seek the Lord.

"Hold fast to love and justice" (v. 6) was a call for the people to respond to God's covenantal love by obeying His will and ways. To hold fast to something expresses an intention to guard, keep, preserve or protect that thing.[3] (Interestingly, this image may also reflect how Jacob held fast to Esau's heel at birth and how he said to God in Genesis 32:26b, *"I will not let you go unless you bless me."*)

Finally, *"wait continually for your God"* in Hosea 12:6 implies placing all faith and hope in the God of Hosts and the security He supplies. The Hebrew word translated as "wait" refers to waiting for God to act; it shows expectation for divine intervention.[4]

Look up the following verses, and record what they tell us about waiting expectantly for God.

· *Psalm 37:9:*

· *Lamentations 3:25:*

· *Isaiah 40:31:*

· *Psalm 25:3:*

What is one thing you can do today to hold fast to God and wait expectantly for Him to act?

Week Five
REFLECTION *and* PRAYER

In Hosea 12:1, the prophet said, *"Ephraim feeds on the wind and pursues the east wind all day long; they multiply falsehood and violence ..."*

Hundreds of years earlier, the writer of Ecclesiastes spoke about *"the wandering of the appetite: this also is vanity and a striving after wind"* (Ecclesiastes 6:9).

From both of these scriptures, it's clear that we may chase after all the world has to offer ... but the only truly meaningful pursuit in life is to seek the Lord and His righteousness.

False sustenance will fade away. We learn a similar lesson when, as children, we experience hunger and always reach for a bag of chips or a cookie — but as adults, we hopefully learn the difference between what will truly satisfy our physical needs and what will not.

Yet somehow, like Israel, we keep trying to feed on the wind when it comes to our spiritual nourishment. Instead of waiting continually on the Lord, we rush ahead in our own ways and with our own strength. Instead of holding fast to love and justice, we grip our plans or our comforts.

Today, let's decide we will no longer fill ourselves with things that will not last. Instead, let's feast on the *"bread of life"* given to us in Christ — and never hunger or thirst again (John 6:35).

Let's pray.

Dear heavenly Father, God of Hosts, expose the pursuits in our lives that are like chasing after the wind. Let us not use all our energy on empty efforts. We don't want to wander aimlessly through life, grasping at abundance that can only be found in You. Forgive us for the times when we've looked for a feast where there is only famine. Let us feast today on the goodness of Your Son and Your Word. In Jesus' name, amen.

"i will betroth you to me forever.
i will betroth you to me
righteousness and in jus
steadfast love and in m
i will betroth you to me
and you shall know the Lo
—Hosea 2:19-2

275   From The D
Psalm 130. 8s and 7s.

1. From the depths do   I   in-voke Thee,
2. Lord, if Thou shouldst mark transgressions
3. For Je - ho - vah   I   am wait - ing,
4. For   the Lord   my   soul is wait-ing M

To my voice be Thou at - ten - tive A
But with Thee there is for-give-ness, T
In His word of   promise giv - en, Y
More than they for morning watching, W

CHORUS

Is - r'el hope thou in Je - ho - vah, Mercies great are found with Him;

irkpatrick

e ear;
word.

hear.
Lord.

I stand?
night,

ommand.
g light..

righteou
steadfas
l will be
faithful

NOTES

NOTES

NOTES

NOTES

Day 26 — Hosea 12:7-14

God guided people through His prophets.

---　❋　---

As we've grown to expect from Hosea, an abrupt shift in metaphor begins today's reading. No longer is the history of Israel's patriarch Jacob in view (Hosea 12:3-5). Hosea now used the metaphor of a dishonest merchant to expose the attitude of the nation's heart (Hosea 12:7-8).

What was the merchant holding, and what did he love, according to Hosea 12:7?

"False balances" (v. 7) refers to how goods were often sold by weight in the Ancient Near East; some greedy sellers sneakily added weight to their scales so people would end up paying more for less product. Hosea likened Ephraim to this kind of merchant, as she boasted in her riches and believed her wrongdoing should be overlooked (Hosea 12:8).

In Hosea's time, Israel experienced economic prosperity — but not because of faithfulness to God's covenant. Like the merchant's, her wealth came from deception and extortion. The poor were cheated and oppressed (Amos 8:4-6). And while it seemed Ephraim's sin had gone unpunished, God answered her boasting in the next verse.

How did God identify Himself in Hosea 12:9? What did God say He would do?

The phrase *"dwell in tents, as in the days of the appointed feast"* (v. 9) recalls the Feast of Booths, a festival that commemorated how God's people had lived after He rescued them from Egypt (Leviticus 23:39-44). Scholars believe God's plan to make His people live in tents again probably had two intentions:

1. The nation who boasted in her riches from dishonest gain would be humbled. Her wealth would be stripped away, and she would be reduced to living in tents in the wilderness.

2. As we've seen previously in Hosea, dwelling in tents would also take Israel back to circumstances where she depended on God for everything and where He tenderly met the needs of His people.[1]

Scholar Thomas McComiskey also sees a parallel structure in Hosea 12:7-10: Verse 9 answers the boasting of the dishonest merchant in verse 7. Verse 10 serves as God's response to the nation's claim to innocence in verse 8.[2]

Specifically, Hosea 12:10 says God repeatedly *"spoke to the prophets ... and through the prophets gave parables"* to remind His people of His covenant and call them to return to a right relationship with Him. The prophets acted as covenant enforcers; therefore, Israel could not ignore the Truth of God's righteous law or avoid the punishment for her rejection of it.

Read Luke 18:9-14. How does verse 9 describe the people to whom Jesus told this parable?

How does Jesus' parable of the Pharisee and the tax collector echo the truth of Hosea 12:7-14? (Note that tax collectors were known for stealing money in Jesus' day, and Pharisees were known for being self-righteous.)

Jesus said whoever exalts himself will be humbled, and whoever humbles himself will be exalted. Elsewhere in Scripture, the Apostles Peter and James reinforced Jesus' charge, imploring Christians to humble themselves and trust that God would lift them up and give them purpose and significance (1 Peter 5:6; James 4:10).

The Message Bible paraphrases the words of James 4:7-10 like this:

"So let God work his will in you. Yell a loud no *to the Devil and watch him make himself scarce. Say a quiet* yes *to God and he'll be there in no time. Quit dabbling in sin. Purify your inner life ... Get down on your knees before the Master; it's the only way you'll get on your feet."*

How can you "say a quiet yes to God" *today by humbling yourself, getting down on your knees before your Master, and letting Him set you on your feet?*

HOSEA 12 *and* REVELATION

In Hosea 12:8, Ephraim said, *"I am rich; I have found wealth for myself; in all my labors they cannot find in me iniquity or sin."*

In Revelation 3:17, we see a prophecy about the church of Laodicea, which God told to repent because the believers there were saying: *"I am rich, I have prospered, and I need nothing."* Similar to the people of Hosea's time, the members of this church did not realize that in God's eyes, their sin actually left them *"wretched, pitiable, poor, blind, and naked."*

Laodicea was a wealthy city and highly self-reliant. The people who lived there likely felt self-sufficient and secure in what they could do for themselves. However, Revelation 3:15-16 exposes the pitiful spiritual state of the church of Laodicea, saying she was *"lukewarm."* The water we drink and use tends to be either hot or cold, both of which are good. Lukewarm water is not good for much and may even be discarded. The church of Laodicea was in a similar spot: not very useful and in danger of judgment.

Still, as we've seen in Hosea, God gave this church the same opportunity He gave Israel. They could trade their faulty, earthly securities for His riches, and like Israel, they could choose to submit to God's discipline and repent (Revelation 3:19). God says in Revelation 3:20, *"Behold, I stand at the door and knock. If anyone hears my voice and opens the door, I will come in to him and eat with him, and he with me."*

As God stands at the door and knocks in Revelation, He knocked on Israel's door through the prophet Hosea, and today He knocks in our hearts too. Let us be those who hear His voice and open the door! Christ's response to a heart that trusts in Him is that He enters and joins us in a meal of fellowship. The sharing of a common meal indicated a strong bond of affection and companionship in the Ancient Near East; today it is also a symbol of the intimacy with Jesus that believers will enjoy in His coming Kingdom.

Here again we see God's love demonstrated through discipline and the urgent call to hear and respond.[1]

Day 27 — Hosea 13:1-8

Hosea demonstrated the absurdity of loving calves but hating people.

———————————— ✦ ————————————

The opening words of Hosea 13 place Ephraim on a pedestal of sorts as a tribe that was once *"exalted in Israel."* Ephraim was indeed formidable: The fact that *"when Ephraim spoke, there was trembling"* (Hosea 13:1) furthers this image, as the Israelites responded as though they were hearing the words of a god (Hosea 10:5). The Hebrew word for *"trembling"* in Hosea 13:1 is only used here in all of Scripture and could also be translated "horror." So not only did the leaders of the nation act wickedly, but the people responded to them wrongly with great fear ... fear they wouldn't have had to experience if they had revered the one true God.

The tribe of Ephraim was regarded as the chief tribe of the western encampment when God's people were in the wilderness (Numbers 2:18-24), and by all accounts, it was still a prominent tribe in Hosea's day.[1] While the focus in Hosea 13 is specifically the tribe of Ephraim, as Hosea has used it throughout the book, the name also represents the nation of Israel as a whole.

Hosea 13:1 says Ephraim *"incurred guilt through Baal and died."* Again, Hosea emphasized one reason for the death of the Israelite nation: They forgot God (v. 6).

What did Hosea say prompted Israel to forget God in verse 6?

The Amplified Bible translation reveals an important nuance in the meaning of this verse: *"When they had their pasture, they became satisfied, And being satisfied, their heart became proud (self-centered); Therefore they forgot Me"* (Hosea 13:6, AMP). Hosea makes it clear that Israel's demise as a nation was caused by her idol worship, and her idol worship was caused by pride.

Maybe the idea of carved images and pagan altars built on hillsides can feel far away from the practices of our current day. Maybe we're tempted to read the prophecy of Hosea as though from a safe distance, believing the problems of God's people in Hosea's time are unrelated to today. Self-centeredness, however, is a problem for all people, including you and me.

In what areas of your life have you experienced a progression similar to Israel's: from satisfaction to self-centeredness to forgetting God?

In Mark 4:1-9, Jesus told a parable to describe His Word and how people receive it. Using a metaphor familiar to His original listeners, He said the Word is like a seed that falls in different places, leading to different outcomes depending on where it lands. For our purposes today, let's focus on the seed that *"fell among thorns, and the thorns grew up and choked it, and it yielded no grain"* (Mark 4:7).

When Jesus explained this parable later in Mark 4, what three things did He say the "thorns" represent, according to Mark 4:18-19?

1.

2.

3.

What did Jesus say is the result of the seed that falls among the thorns (Mark 4:19)?

In Hosea's day, the people of God became enamored with and distracted by what Jesus would call *"the cares of the world and the deceitfulness of riches and the desires for other things"* (Mark 4:19). And the more they forgot God, the more irrational and immoral their lives became. In Hosea 13:2, we even see that the people were willing to *"offer human sacrifice"* yet *"kiss calves"* made of metal. They valued false gods made by humans more than they valued humans made by God.

As we close today's study, consider for a moment how you treat things you want to remember. Maybe you put them on a digital or paper calendar. Maybe you post a note on your refrigerator, a mirror, or the steering wheel of your car. Maybe you ask someone else to help you remember. Whatever measures we take, when we truly don't want to forget something, **we take action to remember it**.

How are you actively taking measures not to forget God and His Word?

Instead of naively assuming we are so different from God's people in the past, let us acknowledge our own forgetfulness and take measures to remember God. Let us cultivate hearts that hear His Word, hold fast to it and bear fruit (Mark 4:20).

God said He removed Israel's king in judgment,
just as He had once put the king on the throne.

Today's reading concludes God's grievances against His people's sins in Hosea.[1] Common themes in the book prevail through the end of Chapter 13, including: the guilt of Israel, the imagery of wilderness and drought, the certainty of defeat and exile, and references to Exodus.

Hosea 13:15 gives us a final reminder that while Ephraim had the *appearance* of flourishing, the people were not rooted in the love and knowledge of God. Therefore, in the day of trouble, they would have no one to rescue them; the kings Israel had asked God for, and in whom they placed their security, would offer them no hope (Hosea 13:10-11).

Long ago, God had used *"a strong east wind"* to part the Red Sea so Israel could escape the Egyptian army (Exodus 14:21), but now God would use *"the east wind, the wind of the LORD"* to dry up Israel's land and pave the way for the Assyrian army to consume them (Hosea 13:15).

What two declarations did God make about what else He "shall" do in Hosea 13:14?

What two questions did He direct toward Death and Sheol (the spiritual place of the dead)?

Scholars debate whether Hosea 13:14 should be interpreted as a negative enforcement of God's judgment for Israel's sin or as a positive interjection of hope for the restoration of Israel (as we've seen since the beginning of the book, like in Hosea 1:6-10). Surrounded by evidence of Israel's sin and unfaithfulness, it might seem out of place for the tone to shift away from judgment; however, it is not uncommon for Hosea to weave oracles of judgment and doom with threads of hope and restoration, and that is likely the case here.[2]

The idea that God would *"ransom them"* in verse 14 carried the idea of transferring ownership. Similarly, to *"redeem"* can mean to gain or regain possession of something.[3] Together these statements emphasize that sin and death had taken possession of God's people — but He would buy them back. In the midst of their turning against Him as their Helper (Hosea 13:9), God still lovingly planned a way for His people to return to Him.

How does this remind us of what we read about Hosea's marriage back in Hosea 3? How does this remind us of the gospel? (Hint: See Mark 10:45.)

The final phrase of Hosea 13:14 (*"compassion is hidden from my eyes"*) reinforced that Hosea's generation would face consequences for abandoning God and rejecting His covenant. Still, their rebellion could not outrun the reach of God's redemption. In fact, the interjection of hope in Hosea 13:14 foretold of a people redeemed.

In 1 Corinthians 15:55, the Apostle Paul would later draw on the questions from Hosea 13:14 to show how Jesus' sacrificial death and resurrection paid the ransom price for our sin, transferring believers from defeat to victory over death.

In 1 Corinthians 15:57-58, what did Paul call Christians to do in response to this victory?

In Hosea's time, God's people proved **not** to have *"steadfast, immovable"* faith like Paul described in 1 Corinthians 15:58. They did **not** *"abound in work of the Lord"*; therefore, all they labored for **was** *"in vain."* In the book of Hosea, we witness the futility of labor not for the Lord.

Today, let us instead throw ourselves onto the mercy of Jesus — and then we can throw ourselves into the work of Jesus and live for His purposes. When we do, we can be sure our labor is not in vain.

Describe a time when you felt like your work was useless or wasted. In light of 1 Corinthians 15:58, what work can you do today that will be useful and valuable in God's Kingdom?

Day 29 — HOSEA 14:1-7

Hosea called Israel to renounce their idols.

The first section of Hosea 14 can be divided into two parts: Israel's confession (Hosea 14:1-3) and God's response (Hosea 14:4-7). The chapter opens with a tone that has again become tender. God not only called for His people to return, but He also showed them the way back.

The phrase *"take with you words"* in verse 2 did not require Israel merely to recite words of confession or prayer to find restoration. Coupled with the plea to *"return to the LORD,"* it also implied turning their hearts toward God in true repentance.[1]

Fill in the blanks of Hosea 14:3 below with the terms of Israel's repentance:

" __________________ shall not save us; we will not __________ on _________; and we will say ______ ____________ 'Our God,' to the work of our hands. In you the orphan finds mercy."

The people needed to repent of worshipping false objects of faith, including other nations, other gods and themselves. This repentance would include a resolution not to rebel against their Father any longer and to say "no more" to man-made idols.

Just as Israel would renounce their misplaced faith and reliance on things that couldn't save them, we, too, can examine our hearts.

Look again at Hosea 14:3. This time, ask God to reveal the things in your heart that fill in the blanks:

_____________________________ *will never save me.*

I will not _____________________________.

I will say "no more" to _____________________________.

The nation of Israel's words of confession would give way to words of praise as they brought God *"the vows of [their] lips"* (Hosea 14:2). In the New Testament, the author of Hebrews later used a similar expression to convey a sacrifice of praise to God: *"Let us continually offer up ... the fruit of lips that acknowledge his name"* (Hebrews 13:15). The picture is of lips that express gratitude from a heart that has experienced God's unconditional love and grace.

Israel's repentance would be met with God's open arms. God would *"heal their apostasy"* and *"love them freely"* (Hosea 14:4). God would restore to them all that had been lost. Through several plant-related metaphors in verses 5-7, Hosea communicated God's promises that encompassed the totality of health for the nation.[2]

In the chart below, record the comparisons Hosea used to communicate God's blessings. (Each verse contains multiple metaphors.)

VERSE	WHAT ISRAEL WOULD BE LIKE	WHAT THEY WOULD EXPERIENCE
Hosea 14:5	The lily, trees of Lebanon	
Hosea 14:6		Spread out, become beautiful
Hosea 14:7		

These verses display Israel as a revived nation reconciled to God. She would be refreshed, rooted and robust as she dwelled within the bounty of the God who loved her. Theologian Derek Kidner observes, "There is nothing stifling or constricting in the divine love expressed here ... it brings life to everything it reaches."[3]

In what areas of your life might you have viewed God or His Word as constricting?

How does this picture of God's people restored to the abundance of His presence change your perspective?

There is no better place to dwell than beneath the shadow of our Lord (Hosea 14:7). The psalmists also knew this well:

"He who dwells in the shelter of the Most High will abide in the shadow of the Almighty" (Psalm 91:1).

"For a day in your courts is better than a thousand elsewhere. I would rather be a doorkeeper in the house of my God than dwell in the tents of wickedness ... No good thing does he withhold from those who walk uprightly" (Psalm 84:10-11).

Day 30 — HOSEA 14:8-9

God warned severely because He desired for
His people to choose rightly and receive blessings.

❉

As we arrive at the last two verses of Hosea, we find God's final, firm and loving assertion of the never-changing truth that He is the only source of fulfillment for the longing of our hearts.

Hosea 14:8 describes God as an *"evergreen cypress"* who consistently provides fruit. As its name suggests, the evergreen tree stays green all year long. There is no season in which all its leaves turn brown and fall off the branches. When applied to God, this metaphor assures us His provision is always available to us — in every circumstance.

Where do you most often find yourself looking for "fruit" (satisfaction, nourishment, fulfillment) other than God's evergreen provision? How does verse 8 encourage you to turn to God to find what you need?

For those who would listen, God's promises left no room for doubt: He was the One who answered His people's prayers and watched over them. And He is the One who hears our prayers and cares for us today.

The whole way through the book of Hosea, the prophet's warnings and pleas fell on many deaf ears — but the final verse of Hosea says, *"Whoever is wise, let him understand these things"* (v. 9). The irony is those who are *"wise in [their] own eyes"* (Proverbs 3:7) do not know the wisdom of God. It is God Himself who gives true wisdom and understanding. So Hosea wasn't saying his prophecies are only for really smart people; they are for people who seek the Lord.

This is why Jesus would later say about the wisdom He shared, *"I thank you, Father, Lord of heaven and earth, that you have hidden these things from the wise and understanding and revealed them to little children"* (Matthew 11:25). Today's verses in Hosea, like many scriptures in God's Word, are designed to awaken a hunger for wisdom in us.

How might you pray for wisdom in alignment with Hosea 14:9?

Duane Garrett says of Hosea 14:8-9, "The text invites the reader to a way of life; it is a path that leads to understanding and to God."[1] God's invitation to His people, then and now, is to walk in His right ways. And today we can accept this invitation by grace through faith in our Savior: Jesus is *"the way, the truth, and the life"* (John 14:6). The other option is to follow ancient Israel's example and stumble in our own ways (Hosea 14:9).

Read Ephesians 5:15-21, which the Apostle Paul wrote many years after Hosea prophesied. What directives did Paul give concerning how to walk by faith?

Read Colossians 2:6-7, and record what else Paul says about the Christian walk.

Like Hosea, Paul knew that to experience true life and avoid the destruction of sin, believers in God need to know Him and walk in His ways. Paul urged Christians to consider carefully how we go about our lives, describing a path on which we pay such close attention to God's will and His ways that our ways become an imitation of His (Ephesians 5:1).

What keywords in Colossians 2:7 remind you of what we read yesterday in Hosea 14:5-7?

The message of Hosea is as piercing today as it was in ancient Israel, and it demands our response. Will we choose to walk as wise believers in God — living rooted in God's Word, assured of His unconditional love, established in our faith, and blossoming with the fruit of His Spirit? Or will we mix *some* of what God says with some of what we desire, making excuses for our sin? May we not totter on the fence of indecision but instead consider what we have to gain from living in right relationship with God. May we know and love the God who answers us, looks after us, and provides for us in abundance.

Use the space below to record your response to God's unconditional love as you've realized it through our study of Hosea.

Week Six
REFLECTION *and* PRAYER

One scholar notes that throughout Hosea's prophecy, his call was not only for God's people to change their ways but for them to acknowledge their waywardness.[1]

How simple this is — yet we seem to complicate it in our own lives.

Even in our desire to right our wrongs, rather than acknowledge our rebellious desires and bring them to the Lord for help, we try to fix it on our own. But at the root of that action remains the same root as ignoring our sin: arrogance. We have never been and will never be capable of fixing our sin apart from Christ.

As God called to His people in the midst of their waywardness long ago, urging them to return to Him, let us turn and run into the loving arms of our Father today. As we have witnessed time and again throughout Hosea, when we run to our Father, we can expect to find Him with His arms open wide, rejoicing to embrace us and draw us near to Him. *"""In [Him] the orphan finds mercy"* (Hosea 14:3b). He loves freely (Hosea 14:4).

"So you, by the help of your God, return, hold fast to love and justice, and wait continually for your God" (Hosea 12:6).

Let's pray.

Oh, Lord, today I pray Your Word back to You from Psalm 36: How precious is Your steadfast love! Your love extends to the heavens, Your faithfulness to the clouds. Let us take refuge in the shadow of Your wings and feast on the abundance of Your house. Let not the foot of arrogance come upon me or the hand of the wicked drive me away. For with You is the fountain of life. In Jesus' name, amen.

"i will betroth you to me forever.
i will betroth you to me in
righteousness and in jus...
steadfast love and in m...
i will betroth you to me...
and you shall know the Lo...
— Hosea 2:19-2...

275   From The D...
Psalm 130. 8s and 7s.

1. From the depths do   I   in-voke Thee,
2. Lord, if Thou shouldst mark transgressions...
3. For   Je - ho - vah   I   am wait - ing, A...
4. For   the Lord my   soul is wait - ing M...

To   my voice be   Thou at - ten - tive A...
But with Thee there is   for - give - ness, Th...
In His word of   promise giv - en, Y...
More than they for morning watching, W...

CHORUS

Is - r'el hope thou   in   Je - ho - vah, Mercies great are found with Him;

righteou...
steadfas...
l will be
faithful

NOTES

NOTES

NOTES

NOTES

ENDNOTES

GETTING TO KNOW HOSEA

1. Elwell, Walter A. and Philip Wesley Comfort. *Tyndale Bible Dictionary*. Wheaton, IL: Tyndale House Publishers, 2001, p. 614.

2. Smith, Billy. "Hosea," *Holman Illustrated Bible Dictionary*. Edited by Chad Brand et al., Nashville, TN: Holman Bible Publishers, 2003, pp. 784-785.

3. "Hosea, Book Of," *Holman Illustrated Bible Dictionary*. Edited by Chad Brand et al., Nashville, TN: Holman Bible Publishers, 2003, p. 785.

TIMELINE OF EVENTS SURROUNDING THE BOOK OF HOSEA

1. Baldwin, Joyce G. "Hosea, Book Of," *New Bible Dictionary*. Edited by D.R.W. Wood et al., Leicester, England; Downers Grove, IL: InterVarsity Press, 1996, pp. 482-483.

GETTING FAMILIAR WITH HOSEA'S PROPHECIES

1. Elwell, Walter A. and Philip Wesley Comfort. *Tyndale Bible Dictionary*. Wheaton, IL: Tyndale House Publishers, 2001, pp. 615-616.

2. Garrett, Duane A. *Hosea, Joel: An Exegetical and Theological Exposition of Holy Scripture*, vol. 19A, The New American Commentary. Nashville: Broadman & Holman Publishers, 1997, pp. 27-29.

3. Baldwin, Joyce G. "Hosea, Book Of," *New Bible Dictionary*. Edited by D.R.W. Wood et al., Leicester, England; Downers Grove, IL: InterVarsity Press, 1996, p. 483.

SYMBOLIC ACTS OF THE PROPHETS

1. "Symbolic Actions of the Prophets," *Faithlife Study Bible*. Edited by John D. Barry et al., Bellingham, WA: Lexham Press, 2012, 2016.

HOSEA'S WRITING STYLE

1. Garrett, Duane A. *Hosea, Joel: An Exegetical and Theological Exposition of Holy Scripture,* vol. 19A, The New American Commentary. Nashville: Broadman & Holman Publishers, 1997, p. 227.

2. Garrett, Duane A. *Hosea, Joel: An Exegetical and Theological Exposition of Holy Scripture*, vol. 19A, The New American Commentary. Nashville: Broadman & Holman Publishers, 1997, pp. 189-190.

3. Garrett, Duane A. *Hosea, Joel: An Exegetical and Theological Exposition of Holy Scripture*, vol. 19A, The New American Commentary. Nashville: Broadman & Holman Publishers, 1997, pp. 97-98.

4. McComiskey, Thomas Edward. "Hosea," *The Minor Prophets: An Exegetical and Expository Commentary*. Grand Rapids, MI: Baker Academic, 2009, pp. 209-210.

HELPFUL KEYWORDS AND CONCEPTS TO KNOW IN HOSEA

1. Manser, Martin H. *Dictionary of Bible Themes: The Accessible and Comprehensive Tool for Topical Studies*. London, England: Martin Manser, 2009.

2. Jones, Michael R. "Apostasy," *Lexham Theological Wordbook,* Lexham Bible Reference Series. Edited by Douglas Mangum et al., Bellingham, WA: Lexham Press, 2014.

3. Baldwin, Joyce G. "Hosea, Book Of," *New Bible Dictionary.* Edited by D.R.W. Wood et al., Leicester, England; Downers Grove, IL: InterVarsity Press, 1996, p. 483.

THEMES OF HOSEA

1. Stuart, Douglas. *Hosea-Jonah,* vol. 31, Word Biblical Commentary. Dallas, TX: Word, Incorporated, 1987, p. 65.

2. Stuart, Douglas. *Hosea-Jonah,* vol. 31, Word Biblical Commentary. Dallas, TX: Word, Incorporated, 1987, p. 54.

3. "Hosea, Book Of," *Holman Illustrated Bible Dictionary.* Edited by Chad Brand et al., Nashville, TN: Holman Bible Publishers, 2003, p. 785.

4. *"yāḏa," Strong's Hebrew Lexicon.* Blue Letter Bible. https://www.blueletterbible.org/lexicon/h3045/esv/wlc/0-17/#lexResults.

5. "Hosea 6:6," *Faithlife Study Bible.* Edited by John D. Barry et al., Bellingham, WA: Lexham Press, 2012, 2016.

WEEK ONE
DAY 1

1. McComiskey, Thomas Edward. "Hosea," *The Minor Prophets: An Exegetical and Expository Commentary.* Grand Rapids, MI: Baker Academic, 2009, p. 10.

2. Garrett, Duane A. *Hosea, Joel: An Exegetical and Theological Exposition of Holy Scripture,* vol. 19A, The New American Commentary. Nashville: Broadman & Holman Publishers, 1997, p. 42.

3. Stuart, Douglas. *Hosea-Jonah,* vol. 31, Word Biblical Commentary. Dallas, TX: Word, Incorporated, 1987, pp. 21-22.

DAY 2

1. Pressler, Carolyn J. "Not My People (Person)," *The Anchor Yale Bible Dictionary.* Edited by David Noel Freedman, New York: Doubleday, 1992, pp. 1136-1137.

2. Stuart, Douglas. *Hosea-Jonah,* vol. 31, Word Biblical Commentary. Dallas, TX: Word, Incorporated, 1987, pp. 33-34.

3. Tripp, Paul David. *New Morning Mercies.* Wheaton, IL: Crossway, 2014.

DAY 3

1. Garrett, Duane A. *Hosea, Joel: An Exegetical and Theological Exposition of Holy Scripture,* vol. 19A, The New American Commentary. Nashville: Broadman & Holman Publishers, 1997, p. 71.

2. Stuart, Douglas. *Hosea-Jonah,* vol. 31, Word Biblical Commentary. Dallas, TX: Word, Incorporated, 1987, pp. 37-38.

DAY 4

1. McComiskey, Thomas Edward. "Hosea," *The Minor Prophets: An Exegetical and Expository Commentary.* Grand Rapids, MI: Baker Academic, 2009, p. 32.

2. Calvin, John. "Hosea 2," *Calvin's Commentaries—Complete.* Text Courtesy of Christian Classics Etherial Library. https://ccel.org/ccel/calvin/calcom26.html.

3. McComiskey, Thomas Edward. "Hosea," *The Minor Prophets: An Exegetical and Expository Commentary.* Grand Rapids, MI: Baker Academic, 2009, p. 34.

DAY 5

1. Henry, Matthew and Thomas Scott. "Hosea 2:6," *Matthew Henry's Concise Commentary.* Oak Harbor, WA: Logos Research Systems, 1997.

2. Garrett, Duane A. *Hosea, Joel: An Exegetical and Theological Exposition of Holy Scripture,* vol. 19A, The New American Commentary. Nashville: Broadman & Holman Publishers, 1997, pp. 84-85.

WEEK TWO
THE WILDERNESS IN SCRIPTURE

1. Garrett, Duane A. *Hosea, Joel: An Exegetical and Theological Exposition of Holy Scripture,* vol. 19A, The New American Commentary. Nashville: Broadman & Holman Publishers, 1997, pp. 89-90.

DAY 7

1. Garrett, Duane A. *Hosea, Joel: An Exegetical and Theological Exposition of Holy Scripture,* vol. 19A, The New American Commentary. Nashville: Broadman & Holman Publishers, 1997, pp. 98-99.

2. "Hosea 3," *Pulpit Commentary.* Bible Hub, https://biblehub.com/commentaries/pulpit/hosea/3.htm.

3. Garrett, Duane A. *Hosea, Joel: An Exegetical and Theological Exposition of Holy Scripture,* vol. 19A, The New American Commentary. Nashville: Broadman & Holman Publishers, 1997, p. 101.

DAY 8

1. Garrett, Duane A. *Hosea, Joel: An Exegetical and Theological Exposition of Holy Scripture,* vol. 19A, The New American Commentary. Nashville: Broadman & Holman Publishers, 1997, pp. 109-110.

DAY 9

1. Garrett, Duane A. *Hosea, Joel: An Exegetical and Theological Exposition of Holy Scripture,* vol. 19A, The New American Commentary. Nashville: Broadman & Holman Publishers, 1997, pp. 121-122.

2. McComiskey, Thomas Edward. "Hosea," *The Minor Prophets: An Exegetical and Expository Commentary.* Grand Rapids, MI: Baker Academic, 2009, p. 66.

3. Stuart, Douglas. *Hosea-Jonah,* vol. 31, Word Biblical Commentary. Dallas, TX: Word, Incorporated, 1987, pp. 71, 81.

DAY 10

1. "Hosea 4," *Pulpit Commentary.* Bible Hub, https://biblehub.com/commentaries/pulpit/hosea/4.htm.

WEEK THREE
DAY 11

1. Garrett, Duane A. *Hosea, Joel: An Exegetical and Theological Exposition of Holy Scripture,* vol. 19A, The New American Commentary. Nashville: Broadman & Holman Publishers, 1997, p. 142.

2. Henry, Matthew and Thomas Scott. "Hosea 5:1," *Matthew Henry's Concise Commentary.* Oak Harbor, WA: Logos Research Systems, 1997.

Day 12

1. Garrett, Duane A. *Hosea, Joel: An Exegetical and Theological Exposition of Holy Scripture,* vol. 19A, The New American Commentary. Nashville: Broadman & Holman Publishers, 1997, pp. 154-155.

Day 13

1. McComiskey, Thomas Edward. "Hosea," *The Minor Prophets: An Exegetical and Expository Commentary.* Grand Rapids, MI: Baker Academic, 2009, p. 88.

2. McComiskey, Thomas Edward. "Hosea," *The Minor Prophets: An Exegetical and Expository Commentary.* Grand Rapids, MI: Baker Academic, 2009, p. 88.

3. McComiskey, Thomas Edward. "Hosea," *The Minor Prophets: An Exegetical and Expository Commentary.* Grand Rapids, MI: Baker Academic, 2009, pp. 88-89.

Day 14

1. Garrett, Duane A. *Hosea, Joel: An Exegetical and Theological Exposition of Holy Scripture,* vol. 19A, The New American Commentary. Nashville: Broadman & Holman Publishers, 1997, p. 160.

2. Garrett, Duane A. *Hosea, Joel: An Exegetical and Theological Exposition of Holy Scripture,* vol. 19A, The New American Commentary. Nashville: Broadman & Holman Publishers, 1997, p. 161.

3. "Hosea 6," *Pulpit Commentary.* Bible Hub, https://biblehub.com/commentaries/pulpit/hosea/6.htm.

WEEK THREE REFLECTION AND PRAYER

1. Henry, Matthew and Thomas Scott. "Hosea 7:1," *Matthew Henry's Concise Commentary.* Oak Harbor, WA: Logos Research Systems, 1997.

WEEK FOUR

Day 16

1. McComiskey, Thomas Edward. "Hosea," *The Minor Prophets: An Exegetical and Expository Commentary.* Grand Rapids, MI: Baker Academic, 2009, p. 112.

Day 17

1. McComiskey, Thomas Edward. "Hosea," *The Minor Prophets: An Exegetical and Expository Commentary.* Grand Rapids, MI: Baker Academic, 2009, pp. 120-121.

2. McComiskey, Thomas Edward. *"*Hosea,*" The Minor Prophets: An Exegetical and Expository Commentary.* Grand Rapids, MI: Baker Academic, 2009, p. 121.

Day 19

1. Garrett, Duane A. *Hosea, Joel: An Exegetical and Theological Exposition of Holy Scripture*, vol. 19A, The New American Commentary. Nashville: Broadman & Holman Publishers, 1997, pp. 192-193.

2. Garrett, Duane A. *Hosea, Joel: An Exegetical and Theological Exposition of Holy Scripture,* vol. 19A, The New American Commentary. Nashville: Broadman & Holman Publishers, 1997, pp. 189-190.

DAY 20

1. Garrett, Duane A. *Hosea, Joel: An Exegetical and Theological Exposition of Holy Scripture,* vol. 19A, The New American Commentary. Nashville: Broadman & Holman Publishers, 1997, pp. 199-200.

2. McComiskey, Thomas Edward. "Hosea," *The Minor Prophets: An Exegetical and Expository Commentary.* Grand Rapids, MI: Baker Academic, 2009, p. 148.

WEEK FIVE

DAY 21

1. McComiskey, Thomas Edward. "Hosea," *The Minor Prophets: An Exegetical and Expository Commentary.* Grand Rapids, MI: Baker Academic, 2009, p. 167.

DAY 22

1. McComiskey, Thomas Edward. "Hosea," *The Minor Prophets: An Exegetical and Expository Commentary.* Grand Rapids, MI: Baker Academic, 2009, p. 178.

2. McComiskey, Thomas Edward. "Hosea," *The Minor Prophets: An Exegetical and Expository Commentary.* Grand Rapids, MI: Baker Academic, 2009, pp. 177-178.

3. Henry, Matthew and Thomas Scott. "Hosea 10:9," *Matthew Henry's Concise Commentary.* Oak Harbor, WA: Logos Research Systems, 1997.

DAY 23

1. McComiskey, Thomas Edward. "Hosea," *The Minor Prophets: An Exegetical and Expository Commentary.* Grand Rapids, MI: Baker Academic, 2009, p. 184.

DAY 24

1. Armstrong, Aaron. "Why Do We Say That God Is Holy?" The Gospel Project, December 4, 2019, https://gospelproject. lifeway.com/god-holy/#:~:text=The%20Hebrew%20word%20for%20%E2%80%9Choly,perfectly%20good%20all%20 the%20time.

2. Henry, Matthew and Thomas Scott. "Hosea 11:8," *Matthew Henry's Concise Commentary.* Oak Harbor, WA: Logos Research Systems, 1997.

3. Barrett, Matthew. "The Immutability and Impassibility of God." The Gospel Coalition, https://www.thegospelcoalition. org/essay/immutability-impassibility-god/.

DAY 25

1. McComiskey, Thomas Edward. "Hosea," *The Minor Prophets: An Exegetical and Expository Commentary.* Grand Rapids, MI: Baker Academic, 2009, p. 200.

2. Garrett, Duane A. *Hosea, Joel: An Exegetical and Theological Exposition of Holy Scripture,* vol. 19A, The New American Commentary. Nashville: Broadman & Holman Publishers, 1997, pp. 237-238.

3. "*šāmar,*" *Strong's Hebrew Lexicon.* Blue Letter Bible, https://www.blueletterbible.org/lexicon/h8104/esv/wlc/0-1/.

4. McComiskey, Thomas Edward. "Hosea," *The Minor Prophets: An Exegetical and Expository Commentary.* Grand Rapids,

MI: Baker Academic, 2009, pp. 202-203.

WEEK SIX
DAY 26

1. McComiskey, Thomas Edward. "Hosea," *The Minor Prophets: An Exegetical and Expository Commentary.* Grand Rapids, MI: Baker Academic, 2009, p. 206.

2. McComiskey, Thomas Edward. "Hosea," *The Minor Prophets: An Exegetical and Expository Commentary.* Grand Rapids, MI: Baker Academic, 2009, pp. 206-207.

   HOSEA 12 AND REVELATION

1. Mounce, Robert H. *The Book of Revelation,* The New International Commentary on the New Testament. Grand Rapids, MI: William B. Eerdmans Publishing Co., 1997, p. 114.

DAY 27

1. McComiskey, Thomas Edward. "Hosea," *The Minor Prophets: An Exegetical and Expository Commentary.* Grand Rapids, MI: Baker Academic, 2009, p. 213.

DAY 28

1. Garrett, Duane A. *Hosea, Joel: An Exegetical and Theological Exposition of Holy Scripture,* vol. 19A, The New American Commentary. Nashville: Broadman & Holman Publishers, 1997, pp. 255-256.

2. Garrett, Duane A. *Hosea, Joel: An Exegetical and Theological Exposition of Holy Scripture,* vol. 19A, The New American Commentary. Nashville: Broadman & Holman Publishers, 1997, p. 265.

3. McComiskey, Thomas Edward. "Hosea," *The Minor Prophets: An Exegetical and Expository Commentary.* Grand Rapids, MI: Baker Academic, 2009, p. 224.

DAY 29

1. McComiskey, Thomas Edward. "Hosea," *The Minor Prophets: An Exegetical and Expository Commentary.* Grand Rapids, MI: Baker Academic, 2009, p. 229.

2. Garrett, Duane A. *Hosea, Joel: An Exegetical and Theological Exposition of Holy Scripture,* vol. 19A, The New American Commentary. Nashville: Broadman & Holman Publishers, 1997, p. 274.

3. Kidner, Derek. "The Way Home: An Exposition of Hosea 14," *Themelios,* vol. 1, no. 2, 1976, pp. 35-36.

DAY 30

1. Garrett, Duane A. *Hosea, Joel: An Exegetical and Theological Exposition of Holy Scripture,* vol. 19A, The New American Commentary. Nashville: Broadman & Holman Publishers, 1997, pp. 281-282.

WEEK SIX REFLECTION AND PRAYER

1. McComiskey, Thomas Edward. "Hosea," *The Minor Prophets: An Exegetical and Expository Commentary.* Grand Rapids, MI: Baker Academic, 2009, p. 232.

NOTES

NOTES

NOTES

NOTES

JOIN OUR NEXT STUDY ...

Rerouted: Following God's Lead Even When We Lose Our Way,

A Study of the Book of Jonah

A STUDY IN THE FIRST 5 APP
STARTING ON JUNE 9, 2025